# ULYSSES

*James Joyce*

EDITORIAL DIRECTOR Laurie Barnett
DIRECTOR OF TECHNOLOGY Tammy Hepps

SERIES EDITOR John Crowther
MANAGING EDITOR Vincent Janoski

WRITER Laura Heffernan
EDITORS John Crowther, Justin Kestler

This edition published by Spark Publishing

Spark Publishing
A Division of SparkNotes LLC
120 Fifth Avenue, 8th Floor
New York, NY 10011

Please submit all comments and questions or report errors to www.sparknotes.com/errors

Printed and bound in the United States

ISBN 1-58663-494-1

# CONTENTS

# CONTEXT

J AMES JOYCE WAS BORN on February 2, 1882, in Dublin, Ireland, into a Catholic middle-class family that would soon become poverty-stricken. Joyce went to Jesuit schools, followed by University College, Dublin, where he began publishing essays. After graduating in 1902, Joyce went to Paris with the intention of attending medical school. Soon afterward, however, he abandoned medical studies and devoted all of his time to writing poetry, stories, and theories of aesthetics. Joyce returned to Dublin the following year when his mother died. He stayed in Dublin for another year, during which time he met his future wife, Nora Barnacle. At this time, Joyce also began work on an autobiographical novel called *Stephen Hero.* Joyce eventually gave up on *Stephen Hero,* but reworked much of the material into *A Portrait of the Artist as a Young Man,* which features the same autobiographical protagonist, Stephen Dedalus, and tells the story of Joyce's youth up to his 1902 departure for Paris.

Nora and Joyce left Dublin again in 1904, this time for good. They spent most of the next eleven years living in Rome and Trieste, Italy, where Joyce taught English and he and Nora had two children, Giorgio and Lucia. In 1907 Joyce's first book of poems, *Chamber Music,* was published in London. He published his book of short stories, *Dubliners,* in 1914, the same year he published *A Portrait of the Artist as a Young Man* in serial installments in the London journal *The Egoist.*

Joyce began writing *Ulysses* in 1914, and when World War I broke out he moved his family to Zurich, Switzerland, where he continued work on the novel. In Zurich, Joyce's fortunes finally improved as his talent attracted several wealthy patrons, including Harriet Shaw Weaver. *Portrait* was published in book form in 1916, and Joyce's play, *Exiles,* in 1918. Also in 1918, the first episodes of *Ulysses* were published in serial form in *The Little Review.* In 1919, the Joyces moved to Paris, where *Ulysses* was published in book form in 1922. In 1923, with his eyesight quickly diminishing, Joyce began working on what became *Finnegans Wake,* published in 1939. Joyce died in 1941.

Joyce first conceived of *Ulysses* as a short story to be included in *Dubliners,* but decided instead to publish it as a long novel, situated as a sort of sequel to *A Portrait of the Artist as a Young Man. Ulysses* picks up Stephen Dedalus's life more than a year after where *Portrait* leaves off. The novel introduces two new main characters, Leopold and Molly Bloom, and takes place on a single day, June 16, 1904, in Dublin.

*Ulysses* strives to achieve a kind of realism unlike that of any novel before it by rendering the thoughts and actions of its main characters—

both trivial and significant—in a scattered and fragmented form similar to the way thoughts, perceptions, and memories actually appear in our minds. In *Dubliners,* Joyce had tried to give his stories a heightened sense of realism by incorporating real people and places into them, and he pursues the same strategy on a massive scale in *Ulysses.* At the same time that *Ulysses* presents itself as a realistic novel, it also works on a mythic level, by way of a series of parallels with Homer's *Odyssey.* Stephen, Bloom, and Molly correspond respectively to Telemachus, Ulysses, and Penelope, and each of the eighteen episodes of the novel corresponds to an adventure from the *Odyssey.*

*Ulysses* has become particularly famous for Joyce's stylistic innovations. In *Portrait,* Joyce first attempted the technique of interior monologue, or stream-of-consciousness. He also experimented with shifting style—the narrative voice of *Portrait* changes stylistically as Stephen matures. In *Ulysses,* Joyce uses interior monologue extensively, and instead of employing one narrative voice, Joyce radically shifts narrative style with each new episode of the novel.

Joyce's early work reveals the stylistic influence of Norwegian playwright Henrik Ibsen. Joyce began reading Ibsen as a young man; his first publication was an article about a play of Ibsen's, which earned him a letter of appreciation from Ibsen himself. Ibsen's plays provided the young Joyce with a model of the realistic depiction of individuals stifled by conventional moral values. Joyce imitated Ibsen's naturalistic brand of realism in *Dubliners, A Portrait of the Artist as a Young Man,* and especially in his play *Exiles. Ulysses* maintains Joyce's concern with realism but also introduces stylistic innovations similar to those of his Modernist contemporaries. *Ulysses*'s multivoiced narration, textual self-consciousness, mythic framework, and thematic focus on life in a modern metropolis situate it close to other main texts of the Modernist movement, such as T. S. Eliot's mythic poem *The Waste Land* (also published in 1922) or Virginia Woolf's stream-of-consciousness novel, *Mrs. Dalloway* (1925).

Though never working in collaboration, Joyce maintained correspondences with other Modernist writers, including Samuel Beckett, and Ezra Pound, who helped find him a patron and an income. Joyce's final work, *Finnegans Wake,* is often seen as bridging the gap between Modernism and postmodernism. A novel only in the loosest sense, *Finnegans Wake* looks forward to postmodern texts in its playful celebration (rather than lamentation) of the fragmentation of experience and the decentered nature of identity, as well as its attention to the non-transparent qualities of language.

Like Eliot and many other Modernist writers, Joyce wrote in self-imposed exile in cosmopolitan Europe. In spite of this fact, all of his work is strongly tied to Irish political and cultural history, and *Ulysses* must also be seen in an Irish context. Joyce's novel was written during the years of the Irish bid for independence from Britain. After a bloody civil war, the Irish Free State was officially formed—during the same year that *Ulysses* was published. Even in 1904, Ireland had experienced the failure of several home rule bills that would have granted the island a measure of political independence within Great Britain. The failure of these bills is linked to the downfall of the Irish member of Parliament, Charles Stewart Parnell, who was once referred to as "Ireland's Uncrowned King," and was publicly persecuted by the Irish church and people in 1889 for conducting a long-term affair with a married woman, Kitty O'Shea. Joyce saw this persecution as an hypocritical betrayal by the Irish that ruined Ireland's chances for a peaceful independence.

Accordingly, *Ulysses* depicts the Irish citizens of 1904, especially Stephen Dedalus, as involved in tangled conceptions of their own Irishness, and complex relationships with various authorities and institutions specific to their time and place: the British empire, Irish nationalism, the Roman Catholic church, and the Irish Literary Revival.

# PLOT OVERVIEW

STEPHEN DEDALUS SPENDS the early morning hours of June 16, 1904, remaining aloof from his mocking friend, Buck Mulligan, and Buck's English acquaintance, Haines. As Stephen leaves for work, Buck orders him to leave the house key and meet them at the pub at 12:30. Stephen resents Buck.

Around 10:00 A.M., Stephen teaches a history lesson to his class at Garrett Deasy's boys' school. After class, Stephen meets with Deasy to receive his wages. The narrow-minded and prejudiced Deasy lectures Stephen on life. Stephen agrees to take Deasy's editorial letter about cattle disease to acquaintances at the newspaper.

Stephen spends the remainder of his morning walking alone on Sandymount Strand, thinking critically about his younger self and about perception. He composes a poem in his head and writes it down on a scrap torn from Deasy's letter.

At 8:00 A.M. the same morning, Leopold Bloom fixes breakfast and brings his wife her mail and breakfast in bed. One of her letters is from Molly's concert tour manager, Blazes Boylan (Bloom suspects he is also Molly's lover)—Boylan will visit at 4:00 this afternoon. Bloom returns downstairs, reads a letter from their daughter, Milly, then goes to the outhouse.

At 10:00 A.M., Bloom picks up an amorous letter from the post office—he is corresponding with a woman named Martha Clifford under the pseudonym Henry Flower. He reads the tepid letter, ducks briefly into a church, then orders Molly's lotion from the pharmacist. He runs into Bantam Lyons, who mistakenly gets the impression that Bloom is giving him a tip on the horse Throwaway in the afternoon's Gold Cup race.

Around 11:00 A.M., Bloom rides with Simon Dedalus (Stephen's father), Martin Cunningham, and Jack Power to the funeral of Paddy Dignam. The men treat Bloom as somewhat of an outsider. At the funeral, Bloom thinks about the deaths of his son and his father.

At noon, we find Bloom at the offices of the *Freeman* newspaper, negotiating an advertisement for Keyes, a liquor merchant. Several idle men, including editor Myles Crawford, are hanging around in the office, discussing political speeches. Bloom leaves to secure the ad. Stephen arrives at the newspaper with Deasy's letter. Stephen and the other men leave for the pub just as Bloom is returning. Bloom's ad negotiation is rejected by Crawford on his way out.

At 1:00 P.M., Bloom runs into Josie Breen, an old flame, and they discuss Mina Purefoy, who is in labor at the maternity hospital. Bloom stops in Burton's restaurant, but he decides to move on to Davy Byrne's for a light lunch. Bloom reminisces about an intimate afternoon with Molly on Howth. Bloom leaves and is walking toward the National Library when he spots Boylan on the street and ducks into the National Museum.

At 2:00 P.M., Stephen is informally presenting his "Hamlet theory" in the National Library to the poet A.E. and the librarians John Eglinton, Best, and Lyster. A.E. is dismissive of Stephen's theory and leaves. Buck enters and jokingly scolds Stephen for failing to meet him and Haines at the pub. On the way out, Buck and Stephen pass Bloom, who has come to obtain a copy of Keyes' ad.

At 4:00 P.M., Simon Dedalus, Ben Dollard, Lenehan, and Blazes Boylan converge at the Ormond Hotel bar. Bloom notices Boylan's car outside and decides to watch him. Boylan soon leaves for his appointment with Molly, and Bloom sits morosely in the Ormond restaurant—he is briefly mollified by Dedalus's and Dollard's singing. Bloom writes back to Martha, then leaves to post the letter.

At 5:00 P.M., Bloom arrives at Barney Kiernan's pub to meet Martin Cunningham about the Dignam family finances, but Cunningham has not yet arrived. The citizen, a belligerent Irish nationalist, becomes increasingly drunk and begins attacking Bloom's Jewishness. Bloom stands up to the citizen, speaking in favor of peace and love over xenophobic violence. Bloom and the citizen have an altercation on the street before Cunningham's carriage carries Bloom away.

Bloom relaxes on Sandymount Strand around sunset, after his visit to Mrs. Dignam's house nearby. A young woman, Gerty MacDowell, notices Bloom watching her from across the beach. Gerty subtly reveals more and more of her legs while Bloom surreptitiously masturbates. Gerty leaves, and Bloom dozes.

At 10:00 P.M., Bloom wanders to the maternity hospital to check on Mina Purefoy. Also at the hospital are Stephen and several of his medical student friends, drinking and talking boisterously about subjects related to birth. Bloom agrees to join them, though he privately disapproves of their revelry in light of Mrs. Purefoy's struggles upstairs. Buck arrives, and the men proceed to Burke's pub. At closing time, Stephen convinces his friend Lynch to go to the brothel section of town and Bloom follows, feeling protective.

Bloom finally locates Stephen and Lynch at Bella Cohen's brothel. Stephen is drunk and imagines that he sees the ghost of his mother—full of rage, he shatters a lamp with his walking stick. Bloom runs after Stephen and finds him in an argument with a British soldier who knocks him out.

Bloom revives Stephen and takes him for coffee at a cabman's shelter to sober up. Bloom invites Stephen back to his house.

Well after midnight, Stephen and Bloom arrive back at Bloom's house. They drink cocoa and talk about their respective backgrounds. Bloom asks Stephen to stay the night. Stephen politely refuses. Bloom sees him out and comes back in to find evidence of Boylan's visit. Still, Bloom is at peace with the world and he climbs into bed, tells Molly of his day and requests breakfast in bed.

After Bloom falls asleep, Molly remains awake, surprised by Bloom's request for breakfast in bed. Her mind wanders to her childhood in Gibraltar, her afternoon of sex with Boylan, her singing career, Stephen Dedalus. Her thoughts of Bloom vary wildly over the course of the monologue, but it ends with a reminiscence of their intimate moment at Howth and a positive affirmation.

# Character List

*Leopold Bloom* A thirty-eight-year-old advertising canvasser in
Dublin. Bloom was raised in Dublin by his Hungarian
Jewish father, Rudolph, and his Irish Catholic mother,
Ellen. He enjoys reading and thinking about science and
inventions and explaining his knowledge to others. Bloom
is compassionate and curious and loves music. He is
preoccupied by his estrangement from his wife, Molly.

*Marion (Molly) Bloom* Leopold Bloom's wife. Molly Bloom is
thirty-three years old, plump with dark coloring, good-
looking, and flirtatious. She is not well-educated, but she
is nevertheless clever and opinionated. She is a
professional singer, raised by her Irish father, Major Brian
Tweedy, in Gibraltar. Molly is impatient with Bloom,
especially about his refusal to be intimate with her since
the death of their son, Rudy, eleven years ago.

*Stephen Dedalus* An aspiring poet in his early twenties. Stephen is
intelligent and extremely well-read, and he likes music. He
seems to exist more for himself, in a cerebral way, than as
a member of a community or even the group of medical
students that he associates with. Stephen was extremely
religious as a child, but now he struggles with issues of
faith and doubt in the wake of his mother's death, which
occurred less than a year ago.

*Malachi (Buck) Mulligan* A medical student and a friend of Stephen.
Buck Mulligan is plump and well-read, and manages to
ridicule nearly everything. He is well-liked by nearly
everyone for his bawdy and witty jokes except Stephen,
Simon, and Bloom.

*Haines* A folklore student at Oxford who is particularly interested
in studying Irish people and culture. Haines is often
unwittingly condescending. He has been staying at the
Martello tower where Stephen and Buck live.

*Hugh ("Blazes") Boylan* The manager for Molly's upcoming concert in Belfast. Blazes Boylan is well-known and well-liked around town, though he seems somewhat sleazy, especially toward women. Boylan has become interested in Molly, and they commence an affair during the afternoon of the novel.

*Millicent (Milly) Bloom* Molly and Leopold Bloom's fifteen-year-old daughter, who does not actually appear in *Ulysses*. The Blooms recently sent Milly to live in Mullingar and learn photography. Milly is blond and pretty and has become interested in boys—she is dating Alec Bannon in Mullingar.

*Simon Dedalus* Stephen Dedalus's father. Simon Dedalus grew up in Cork, moved to Dublin, and was a fairly successful man until recently. Other men look up to him, even though his home life has been in disarray since his wife died. Simon has a good singing voice and a talent for funny stories, and he might have capitalized on these assets if not for his drinking habit. Simon is extremely critical of Stephen.

*A.E. (George Russell)* A.E. is the pseudonym of George Russell, a famous poet of the Irish Literary Revival who is at the center of Irish literary circles—circles that do not include Stephen Dedalus. He is deeply interested in esoteric mysticism. Other men consult A.E. for wisdom as if he were an oracle.

*Richard Best* A librarian at the National Library. Best is enthusiastic and agreeable, though most of his own contributions to the Hamlet conversation in Episode Nine are points of received wisdom.

*Edy Boardman* One of Gerty MacDowell's friends. Gerty's uppity demeanor annoys Edy, who attempts to deflate Gerty with jibes.

*Josie (née Powell) and Denis Breen* Josie Powell and Bloom were interested in each other when they were younger. Josie was good-looking and flirtatious. After Bloom married Molly, Josie married Denis. Denis Breen is slightly insane and seems paranoid. Looking after her "dotty" husband has taken its toll on Josie, who now seems haggard.

*Cissy, Jacky, and Tommy Caffrey*  Cissy Caffrey is one of Gerty MacDowell's best friends. She is something of a tomboy and quite frank. She looks after her younger toddler brothers, Jacky and Tommy.

*The citizen*  An older Irish patriot who champions the Nationalist cause. Though the citizen seems to work for the cause in no official capacity, others look to him for news and opinions. He was formerly an athlete in Irish sports. He is belligerent and xenophobic.

*Martha Clifford*  A woman with whom Bloom corresponds under the pseudonym Henry Flower. Martha's letters are strewn with spelling mistakes, and she is sexually daring in only a pedestrian way.

*Bella Cohen*  A conniving brothel-mistress. Bella Cohen is large and slightly mannish, with dark coloring. She is somewhat concerned about respectability, and has a son at Oxford, whose tuition is paid by one of her customers.

*Martin Cunningham*  A leader among Bloom's circle of friends. Martin Cunningham can be sympathetic toward others, and he sticks up for Bloom at various points during the day, yet he still treats Bloom as an outsider. He has a face that resembles Shakespeare's.

*Garrett Deasy*  Headmaster of the boys' school where Stephen teaches. Deasy is a Protestant from the north of Ireland, and he is respectful of the English government. Deasy is condescending to Stephen and not a good listener. His overwrought letter to the editor about foot-and-mouth disease among cattle is the object of mockery among Dublin men for the rest of the day.

*Dilly, Katey, Boody, and Maggy Dedalus*  Stephen's younger sisters. They try to keep the Dedalus household running after their mother's death. Dilly seems to have aspirations, such as learning French.

CHARACTER LIST

*Patrick Dignam, Mrs. Dignam, and Patrick Dignam, Jr.* Patrick Dignam is an acquaintance of Bloom who passed away very recently, apparently from drinking. His funeral is today, and Bloom and others get together to raise some money for the widow Dignam and her children, who were left with almost nothing after Paddy used his life insurance to pay off a debt.

*Ben Dollard* A man known around Dublin for his superior bass voice. Ben Dollard's business and career went under a while ago. He seems good-natured but is perhaps rattled by a past drinking habit.

*John Eglinton* An essayist who spends time at the National Library. John Eglinton is affronted by Stephen's youthful self-confidence and doubtful of Stephen's Hamlet theory.

*Richie, Sara (Sally), and Walter Goulding* Richie Goulding is Stephen Dedalus's uncle; he was Stephen's mother, May's, brother. Richie is a law clerk, who has been less able to work recently because of a bad back—a fact that makes him an object of ridicule for Simon Dedalus. Richie and Sara's son, Walter, is "skeweyed" and has a stutter.

*Zoe Higgins* A prostitute in Bella Cohen's brothel. Zoe is outgoing and good at teasing.

*Joe Hynes* A reporter for the Dublin newspaper who seems to be without money often—he borrowed three pounds from Bloom and has not paid him back. Hynes does not know Bloom well, and he appears to be good friends with the citizen in Episode Twelve.

*Corny Kelleher* An undertaker's assistant who is friendly with the police.

*Mina Kennedy and Lydia Douce* The barmaids at the Ormond hotel. Mina and Lydia are flirtatious and friendly to the men who come into the bar, though they tend to be scornful of the opposite sex when they talk together. Miss Douce, who is bronze-haired, seems to be the more outgoing of the two, and she has a crush on Blazes Boylan. Miss Kennedy, who is golden-haired, is more reserved.

*Ned Lambert* A friend of Simon Dedalus and other men in Dublin. Ned Lambert is often found joking and laughing. He works in a seed and grain warehouse downtown, in what used to be St. Mary's Abbey.

*Lenehan* A racing editor at the Dublin newspaper, though his tip, Sceptre, loses the Gold Cup horserace. Lenehan is a jokester and flirtatious with women. He is mocking of Bloom but respectful of Simon and Stephen Dedalus.

*Lynch* A medical student and old friend of Stephen (he also appears in *A Portrait of the Artist as a Young Man*). Lynch is used to hearing Stephen's pretentious and overwhelming aesthetic theories, and he is familiar with Stephen's stubbornness. He is seeing Kitty Ricketts.

*Thomas W. Lyster* A librarian at the National Library in Dublin, and a Quaker. Lyster is the most solicitous of Stephen's listeners in Episode Nine.

*Gerty MacDowell* A woman in her early twenties from a lower-middle-class family. Gerty suffers from a permanent limp, possibly from a bicycle accident. She fastidiously attends to her clothing and personal beauty regimen, and she hopes to fall in love and marry. She rarely allows herself to think about her disability.

*John Henry Menton* A solicitor in Dublin who employed Paddy Dignam. When Bloom and Molly were first courting, Menton was a rival for Molly's affections. He is disdainful of Bloom.

*Episode Twelve's Nameless Narrator* The unnamed narrator of Episode Twelve is currently a debt collector, though this is the most recent of many different jobs. He enjoys feeling like he is "in the know" and has gotten most of his gossip about the Blooms from his friend "Pisser" Burke, who knew them when they lived at the City Arms Hotel.

*City Councillor Nannetti* A head printer for the Dublin newspaper, and a member of Parliament. Nannetti is of mixed Italian and Irish heritage.

*J. J. O'Molloy* A lawyer who is now out of work and money. O'Molloy is thwarted in his attempts to borrow money from friends today. He sticks up for Bloom in Barney Kiernan's pub in Episode Twelve.

*Jack Power* A friend of Simon Dedalus and Martin Cunningham and other men around town. Power possibly works in law enforcement. He is not very nice to Bloom.

*Kitty Ricketts* One of the prostitutes working in Bella Cohen's brothel. Kitty seems to have a relationship with Lynch and has spent part of the day with him. She is thin, and her clothing reflects her upper-class aspirations.

*Florry Talbot* One of the prostitutes in Bella Cohen's brothel. Florry is plump and seems slow but eager to please.

# ANALYSIS OF MAJOR
# CHARACTERS

## LEOPOLD BLOOM

Leopold Bloom functions as a sort of Everyman—a bourgeois Odysseus for the twentieth century. At the same time, the novel's depiction of his personality is one of the most detailed in all literature. Bloom is a thirty-eight-year-old advertising canvasser. His father was a Hungarian Jew, and Joyce exploits the irony of this fact—that Dublin's latter-day Odysseus is really a Jew with Hungarian origins—to such an extent that readers often forget Bloom's Irish mother and multiple baptisms. Bloom's status as an outsider, combined with his own ability to envision an inclusive state, make him a figure who both suffers from and exposes the insularity of Ireland and Irishness in 1904. Yet the social exclusion of Bloom is not simply one-sided. Bloom is clear-sighted and mostly unsentimental when it comes to his male peers. He does not like to drink often or to gossip, and though he is always friendly, he is not sorry to be excluded from their circles.

When Bloom first appears in Episode Four of *Ulysses,* his character is noteworthy for its differences from Stephen's character, on which the first three episodes focus. Stephen's cerebrality makes Bloom's comfort with the physical world seem more remarkable. This ease accords with his practical mind and scientific curiosity. Whereas Stephen, in Episode Three, shuts himself off from the material world to ponder the workings of his own perception, Bloom appears in the beginning of Episode Four bending down to his cat, wondering how *her* senses work. Bloom's comfort with the physical also manifests itself in his sexuality, a dimension mostly absent from Stephen's character. We get ample evidence of Bloom's sexuality—from his penchant for voyeurism and female underclothing to his masturbation and erotic correspondence—while Stephen seems inexperienced and celibate.

Other disparities between the two men further define Bloom's character: where Stephen is depressive and somewhat dramatic, Bloom is mature and even-headed. Bloom possesses the ability to cheer himself up and to pragmatically refuse to think about depressing topics. Yet Bloom and Stephen are similar, too. They are both unrealized artists, if with completely different agendas. As one Dubliner puts it, "There's a touch of the artist about old Bloom." We might say that Bloom's conception of art is bourgeois, in the sense that he considers art as a way to effect people's actions and feelings in an immediate way. From his desire to create a newer, better advertisement, to his love poem to Molly, to his reading of Shakespeare for its moral value, Bloom's version of art does not stray far from real-life situations. Bloom's sense of culture and his aspiration to be "cultured" also seem to bring him close to Stephen. The two men share a love for music, and Stephen's companionship is attractive to Bloom, who would love to be an expert, rather than a dabbler, in various subjects.

Two emotional crises plague Bloom's otherwise cheerful demeanor throughout *Ulysses*—the breakdown of his male family line and the infidelity of his wife, Molly. The untimely deaths of both Bloom's father (by suicide) and only son, Rudy (days after his birth), lead Bloom to feel cosmically lonely and powerless. Bloom is allowed a brief respite from these emotions during his union with Stephen in the latter part of the novel. We slowly realize over the course of *Ulysses* that the first crisis of family line is related to the second crisis of marital infidelity: the Blooms' intimacy and attempts at procreation have broken down since the death of their only son eleven years ago. Bloom's reaction to Molly's decision to look elsewhere (to Blazes Boylan) for sex is complex. Bloom enjoys the fact that other men appreciate his wife, and he is generally a passive, accepting person. Bloom is clear-sighted enough to realize, though, that Blazes Boylan is a paltry replacement for himself, and he ultimately cheers himself by recontextualizing the problem. Boylan is only one of many, and it is on Molly that Bloom should concentrate his own energies.

In fact, it is this ability to shift perspective by sympathizing with another viewpoint that renders Bloom heroic. His compassion is evident throughout—he is charitable to animals and people in need, his sympathies extend even to a woman in labor. Bloom's masculinity is frequently called into question by other characters; hence, the second irony of *Ulysses* is that Bloom as Everyman is also somewhat feminine. And it is precisely his fluid, androgynous capacity to empathize with people and things of all types—and to be both a symbolic father and a mother to Stephen—that makes him the hero of the novel.

## MOLLY BLOOM

Over the course of the novel, we get a very clear picture of Bloom and Stephen because we witness their interactions with many different people and see what they are thinking throughout all of these interactions. For most of the novel we only see Molly Bloom through other people's eyes, so it may be tempting to dismiss her as a self-centered, unfaithful woman. The way we decide to view her will require us to reevaluate the understanding we have thus far formed of Leopold Bloom. If we focus on the "vulgarity" and physicality of her monologue, our built-up sympathies with Bloom as the well-meaning husband of a loose woman are ratified. But a more nuanced understanding of her involves seeing her as an outgoing woman who takes a certain pride in her husband, but who has been feeling a lack of demonstrative love. This idea yields a reevaluation of Bloom as being unfaithful in his own ways and complicit in the temporary breakdown of their marriage.

Like Bloom, Molly is a Dublin outsider. She was raised in the military atmosphere of Gibraltar by her father, Major Brian Tweedy. Molly never knew her mother, who was possibly Jewish, or just Jewish-looking. Bloom associates Molly with the "hot-blooded" Mediterranean regions, and, to a lesser degree, the exoticism of the East. Yet Molly considers her own childhood to have been normal, outside the dramatic entrances and exits of young, good-looking soldiers going off to war. Molly seems to organize her life around men and to have very few female friends. She enjoys being looked at and gains self-esteem from the admiration of men. Molly is extremely self-aware and perceptive—she knows without looking when she is being looked at. A man's admiration of her does not cloud her own negative judgments about him. She is frank about topics that other people are likely to sentimentalize—intimacy, mourning, and motherhood, for example. She is also frank about the extent to which living involves adaptations of different roles. Her sense of this truth—which is perhaps related to her own career as a stage singer—aligns her with Stephen, who is also conscious of his outward existence in terms of a series of roles. Molly and Stephen both share a capacity for storytelling, scene-setting, and mimicry. Molly's storytelling and frankness about role-playing evinces her sense of humor, and it also mediates our sense of her as a hypocritical character. Finally, it is this pragmatic and fluid adoption of roles that enables Molly to reconnect with Bloom through vivid recollections, and, indeed, reenactments, of the past, as in her final memory of the Howth scene at the end of *Ulysses*.

## STEPHEN DEDALUS

The character of Stephen Dedalus is a harshly drawn version of Joyce himself at age twenty-two. Stephen first appeared as the main character of *A Portrait of the Artist as a Young Man,* which followed his development from early childhood to his proud and ambitious days before leaving Dublin for Paris and the realization of his artistic capabilities. When we meet Stephen again at the beginning of *Ulysses,* it is over two years after the end of *Portrait.* Stephen has been back in Dublin for over a year, having returned to sit at his mother's deathbed. Stephen's artistic talent is still unrealized—he is currently a reluctant teacher of history at a boy's school. He is disappointed and moody and is still dressed in mourning over the death of his mother almost a year ago. Stephen's interactions with various characters—Buck, Haines, Mr. Deasy—in the opening episodes of the book crystallize our sense of the damaging ties and obligations that have resulted from Stephen's return to Ireland. At the beginning of *Ulysses,* Stephen is a self-conscious young man whose identity is still in formation. Stephen's aloofness and his attempts to understand himself through fictional characters such as Hamlet dramatize his struggle to solidify this identity.

Stephen is depicted as above most of the action of the novel. He exists mainly within his own world of ideas—his actions in the world tend to pointedly distance himself from others and from the world itself. His freeness with money is less a demonstration of his generosity than of his lack of material concerns. His unwashed state similarly reflects his removal from the material world. His cryptic stories and riddles cut others off rather than include them. He stubbornly holds grudges, and our admiration of his noble struggle for independence is tempered by our knowledge of the impoverished siblings he has left behind. If Stephen himself is an unsympathetic character, however, the issues central to his identity struggle are easier for us to sympathize with. From his contemplation of the eye's perception of the outside world to his teaching of a history lesson to his meditations on *amor matris* or "mother love," Stephen's mental meanderings center on the problem of whether, and how, to be an active or passive being within the world.

Stephen's struggles tend to center around his parents. His mother, who seems to blame Stephen for refusing to pray at her deathbed, represents not only a mother's love but also the church and Ireland. Stephen is haunted by his mother's memory and ghost in the same ways that he is haunted by memories of his early piety. Though Stephen's father is still alive and well, we see Stephen attempting to ignore or deny him throughout all of *Ulysses*. Stephen's struggle with his father seems to be about Stephen's need to have a space in which to create—a space untainted by Simon Dedalus's overly critical judgments. Stephen's struggle to define his identity without the constraint or aid imposed by his father bleeds into larger conflicts—Stephen's struggle with the authority of God, the authority of the British empire, even with the authority of the mocker or joker.

After the first three episodes, Stephen's appearances in *Ulysses* are limited. However, these limited appearances—in Episodes Nine, Fourteen, and Fifteen—demonstrate that Stephen's attempted repudiation of authority and obligations has precipitated what seems to him to be the abandonment of all those close to him. At the end of Episode Fifteen, Stephen lies nearly unconscious on the ground, feeling as though he has been "betrayed" by everyone. Never before has Stephen seemed so much in need of a parent, and it is Bloom—not wholly father nor mother—who cares for him.

Though Stephen plays a part in the final episodes of *Ulysses,* we see less and less of his thoughts as the novel progresses (and, perhaps not coincidentally, Stephen becomes drunker and drunker). Instead, the circumstances of the novel and the apparent choices that Stephen makes take over our sense of his character. By the novel's end, we see that Stephen recognizes a break with Buck Mulligan, will quit his job at Deasy's school, and has accepted, if only temporarily, Bloom's hospitality. In Bloom's kitchen, Stephen puts something in his mouth besides alcohol for the first time since Episode One, and has a conversation with Bloom, as opposed to performing as he did earlier in the day. We are thus encouraged to understand that, in the calm of the late-night hours, Stephen has recognized the power of a reciprocal relationship to provide sustenance.

CHARACTER ANALYSIS

# THEMES, MOTIFS & SYMBOLS

## THEMES

*Themes are the fundamental and often universal ideas explored in a literary work.*

### THE QUEST FOR PATERNITY

At its most basic level, *Ulysses* is a book about Stephen's search for a symbolic father and Bloom's search for a son. In this respect, the plot of *Ulysses* parallels Telemachus's search for Odysseus, and vice versa, in *The Odyssey*. Bloom's search for a son stems at least in part from his need to reinforce his identity and heritage through progeny. Stephen already has a biological father, Simon Dedalus, but considers him a father only in "flesh." Stephen feels that his own ability to mature and become a father himself (of art or children) is restricted by Simon's criticism and lack of understanding. Thus Stephen's search involves finding a symbolic father who will, in turn, allow Stephen himself to be a father. Both men, in truth, are searching for paternity as a way to reinforce their own identities.

Stephen is more conscious of his quest for paternity than Bloom, and he mentally recurs to several important motifs with which to understand paternity. Stephen's thinking about the Holy Trinity involves, on the one hand, Church doctrines that uphold the unity of the Father and the Son and, on the other hand, the writings of heretics that challenge this doctrine by arguing that God created the rest of the Trinity, concluding that each subsequent creation is inherently different. Stephen's second motif involves his Hamlet theory, which seeks to prove that Shakespeare represented himself through the ghost-father in *Hamlet*, but also—through his translation of his life into art—became the father of his own father, of his life, and "of all his race." The Holy Trinity and Hamlet motifs reinforce our sense of Stephen's and Bloom's parallel quests for paternity. These quests seem to end in Bloom's kitchen, with Bloom recognizing "the future" in Stephen and Stephen recognizing "the past" in Bloom. Though united as father and son in this moment, the men will soon part ways, and their paternity quests will undoubtedly continue, for *Ulysses* demonstrates that the quest for paternity is a search for a lasting manifestation of self.

18

## THE REMORSE OF CONSCIENCE

The phrase *agenbite of inwit,* a religious term meaning "remorse of conscience," comes to Stephen's mind again and again in *Ulysses.* Stephen associates the phrase with his guilt over his mother's death—he suspects that he may have killed her by refusing to kneel and pray at her sickbed when she asked. The theme of remorse runs through *Ulysses* to address the feelings associated with modern breaks with family and tradition. Bloom, too, has guilty feelings about his father because he no longer observes certain traditions his father observed, such as keeping kosher. Episode Fifteen, "Circe," dramatizes this remorse as Bloom's "Sins of the Past" rise up and confront him one by one. *Ulysses* juxtaposes characters who experience remorse with characters who do not, such as Buck Mulligan, who shamelessly refers to Stephen's mother as "beastly dead," and Simon Dedalus, who mourns his late wife but does not regret his treatment of her. Though remorse of conscience can have a repressive, paralyzing effect, as in Stephen's case, it is also vaguely positive. A self-conscious awareness of the past, even the sins of the past, helps constitute an individual as an ethical being in the present.

## COMPASSION AS HEROIC

In nearly all senses, the notion of Leopold Bloom as an epic hero is laughable—his job, talents, family relations, public relations, and private actions all suggest his utter ordinariness. It is only Bloom's extraordinary capacity for sympathy and compassion that allows him an unironic heroism in the course of the novel. Bloom's fluid ability to empathize with such a wide variety of beings—cats, birds, dogs, dead men, vicious men, blind men, old ladies, a woman in labor, the poor, and so on—is the modern-day equivalent to Odysseus's capacity to adapt to a wide variety of challenges. Bloom's compassion often dictates the course of his day and the novel, as when he stops at the river Liffey to feed the gulls or at the hospital to check on Mrs. Purefoy. There is a network of symbols in *Ulysses* that present Bloom as Ireland's savior, and his message is, at a basic level, to "love." He is juxtaposed with Stephen, who would also be Ireland's savior but is lacking in compassion. Bloom returns home, faces evidence of his cuckold status, and slays his competition—not with arrows, but with a refocused perspective that is available only through his fluid capacity for empathy.

## PARALLAX, OR THE NEED FOR MULTIPLE PERSPECTIVES

*Parallax* is an astronomical term that Bloom encounters in his reading and that arises repeatedly through the course of the novel. It refers to the difference of position of one object when seen from two different vantage points. These differing viewpoints can be collated to better approximate the position of the object. As a novel, *Ulysses* uses a similar tactic. Three main characters—Stephen, Bloom, and Molly—and a subset of narrative techniques that affect our perception of events and characters combine to demonstrate the fallibility of one single perspective. Our understanding of particular characters and events must be continually revised as we consider further perspectives. The most obvious example is Molly's past love life. Though we can construct a judgment of Molly as a loose woman from the testimonies of various characters in the novel—Bloom, Lenehan, Dixon, and so on—this judgment must be revised with the integration of Molly's own final testimony.

## MOTIFS

*Motifs are recurring structures, contrasts, or literary devices that can help to develop and inform the text's major themes.*

### LIGHTNESS AND DARKNESS
The traditional associations of light with good and dark with bad are upended in *Ulysses,* in which the two protagonists are dressed in mourning black, and the more menacing characters are associated with light and brightness. This reversal arises in part as a reaction to Mr. Deasy's anti-Semitic judgment that Jews have "sinned against the light." Deasy himself is associated with the brightness of coins, representing wealth without spirituality. "Blazes" Boylan, Bloom's nemesis, is associated with brightness through his name and his flashy behavior, again suggesting surface without substance. Bloom's and Stephen's dark colors suggest a variety of associations: Jewishness, anarchy, outsider/wanderer status. Furthermore, Throwaway, the "dark horse," wins the Gold Cup Horserace.

### THE HOME USURPED
While Odysseus is away from Ithaca in *The Odyssey,* his household is usurped by would-be suitors of his wife, Penelope. This motif translates directly to *Ulysses* and provides a connection between Stephen and Bloom. Stephen pays the rent for the Martello tower, where he, Buck, and Haines are staying. Buck's demand of the house key is thus a usurpation of Stephen's household rights, and Stephen recognizes this and refuses to return to the tower. Stephen mentally dramatizes this usurpation as a replay of Claudius's usurpation of Gertrude and the throne in *Hamlet*. Meanwhile, Bloom's home has been usurped by Blazes Boylan, who comes and goes at will and has sex with Molly in Bloom's absence. Stephen's and Bloom's lack of house keys throughout *Ulysses* symbolizes these usurpations.

### THE EAST
The motif of the East appears mainly in Bloom's thoughts. For Bloom, the East is a place of exoticism, representing the promise of a paradisiacal existence. Bloom's hazy conception of this faraway land arises from

a network of connections: the planter's companies (such as Agendeth Netaim), which suggest newly fertile and potentially profitable homes; Zionist movements for a homeland; Molly and her childhood in Gibraltar; narcotics; and erotics. For Bloom and the reader, the East becomes the imaginative space where hopes can be realized. The only place where Molly, Stephen, and Bloom all meet is in their parallel dreams of each other the night before, dreams that seem to be set in an Eastern locale.

# SYMBOLS

*Symbols are objects, characters, figures, or colors used to represent abstract ideas or concepts.*

## PLUMTREE'S POTTED MEAT

In Episode Five, Bloom reads an ad in his newspaper: "What is home without / Plumtree's Potted Meat? / Incomplete. / With it an abode of bliss." Bloom's conscious reaction is his belief that the ad is poorly placed—directly below the obituaries, suggesting an infelicitous relation between dead bodies and "potted meat." On a subconscious level, however, the figure of Plumtree's Potted Meat comes to stand for Bloom's anxieties about Boylan's usurpation of his wife and home. The image of meat inside a pot crudely suggests the sexual relation between Boylan and Molly. The wording of the ad further suggests, less concretely, Bloom's masculine anxieties—he worries that he is not the head of an "abode of bliss" but rather a servant in a home "incomplete." The connection between Plumtree's meat and Bloom's anxieties about Molly's unhappiness and infidelity is driven home when Bloom finds crumbs of the potted meat that Boylan and Molly shared earlier in his own bed.

## THE GOLD CUP HORSERACE

The afternoon's Gold Cup Horserace and the bets placed on it provide much of the public drama in *Ulysses,* though it happens offstage. In Episode Five, Bantam Lyons mistakenly thinks that Bloom has tipped him off to the horse "Throwaway," the dark horse with a long-shot chance. "Throwaway" does end up winning the race, notably ousting "Sceptre," the horse with the phallic name, on which Lenehan and Boylan have bet. This underdog victory represents Bloom's eventual unshowy triumph over Boylan, to win the "Gold Cup" of Molly's heart.

## STEPHEN'S LATIN QUARTER HAT

Stephen deliberately conceives of his Latin Quarter hat as a symbol. The Latin Quarter is a student district in Paris, and Stephen hopes to suggest his exiled, anti-establishment status while back in Ireland. He also refers to the hat as his "Hamlet hat," tipping us off to the intentional brooding and artistic connotations of the head gear. Yet Stephen cannot always control his own hat as a symbol, especially in the eyes of others. Through the eyes of others, it comes to signify Stephen's mock priestliness and provinciality.

### BLOOM'S POTATO TALISMAN

In Episode Fifteen, Bloom's potato functions like Odysseus's use of "moly" in Circe's den—it serves to protect him from enchantment, enchantments to which Bloom succumbs when he briefly gives it over to Zoe Higgins. The potato, old and shriveled now, is an heirloom from Bloom's mother, Ellen. As an organic product that is both fruit and root but is now shriveled, it gestures toward Bloom's anxieties about fertility and his family line. Most important, however, is the potato's connection to Ireland—Bloom's potato talisman stands for his frequently overlooked maternal Irish heritage.

# Summary & Analysis

## Episode One: "Telemachus"

### Summary

It is around 8:00 in the morning, and Buck Mulligan, performing a mock mass with his shaving bowl, calls Stephen Dedalus up to the roof of the Martello tower overlooking Dublin bay. Stephen is unresponsive to Buck's aggressive joking—he is annoyed about Haines, the Englishman whom Buck has invited to stay in the tower. Stephen was awakened during the night by Haines's moaning about a nightmare involving a black panther.

Mulligan and Stephen look out over the sea, which Buck refers to as a great mother. This reminds Mulligan of his aunt's grudge against Stephen for Stephen's refusal to pray at his own mother's deathbed. Stephen, who is still dressed in mourning, looks at the sea and thinks of his mother's death, as Buck mocks Stephen for his second-hand clothes and dirty appearance. Buck holds out a cracked mirror for Stephen to see himself in. Stephen staves off Buck's condescension by suggesting that such a "cracked lookingglass of a servant" could serve as a symbol for Irish art. Buck puts a conciliatory arm around Stephen and suggests that together, they could make Ireland as cultured as Greece once was. Buck offers to terrorize Haines if he annoys Stephen further and Stephen remembers Buck's "ragging" of one of their classmates, Clive Kempthorpe.

Buck asks Stephen about his quiet brooding, and Stephen finally admits to his own grudge against Buck—months ago, Stephen overheard Buck referring to his mother as "beastly dead." Buck tries to defend himself, then gives up and urges Stephen to stop brooding over his own pride.

Buck goes down into the tower singing, unknowingly, the song that Stephen sang to his dying mother. Stephen feels as though he is haunted by his dead mother or the memory of her. Buck calls Stephen downstairs for breakfast. He encourages Stephen to ask Haines, who is impressed with Stephen's Irish wit, for money, but Stephen refuses. Stephen goes down to the kitchen and helps Buck serve breakfast. Haines announces that the milk woman is approaching. Buck makes a joke about "old mother Grogan" making tea and making water (urine), and encourages Haines to use it for a book of Irish folk life.

The milk woman enters, and Stephen imagines her as a symbol of Ireland. Stephen is silently bitter that the milk woman respects Buck, a medical student, more than him. Haines speaks Irish to her, but she does not understand and thinks he is speaking French. Buck pays her and she leaves.

Haines announces his desire to make a book of Stephen's sayings, but Stephen asks if he would make money off it. Haines walks outside, and Buck scolds Stephen for being rude and ruining their chances of getting drinking money from Haines. Buck dresses and the three men walk down toward the water. On the way, Stephen explains that he rents the tower from the secretary of state for war. Haines asks Stephen about his Hamlet theory, but Buck insists it wait until they have drinks later. Haines explains that their Martello tower reminds him of Hamlet's Elsinore. Buck interrupts Haines to run ahead, dancing and singing "The Ballad of Joking Jesus." Haines and Stephen walk together. As Haines talks, Stephen anticipates that Buck will ask Stephen for the key to the tower—the tower for which Stephen pays the rent. Haines questions Stephen about his religious beliefs. Stephen explains that two masters, England and the Catholic Church, stand in the way of his free-thinking, and a third master, Ireland, wants him for "odd jobs." Trying to be conciliatory about Irish servitude to the British, Haines weakly offers, "It seems history is to blame." Haines and Stephen stand overlooking the bay and Stephen remembers a man who recently drowned.

Haines and Stephen walk down to the water where Buck is getting undressed, and two others, including a friend of Buck's, are already swimming. Buck talks to his friend about their mutual friend, Bannon, who is in Westmeath—Bannon apparently has a girlfriend (we learn later she is Milly Bloom). Buck gets in the water, while Haines smokes, digesting. Stephen announces that he is leaving, and Buck demands the tower key and two pence for a pint. Buck tells Stephen to meet him at a pub—The Ship—at 12:30. Stephen walks away, vowing that he will not return to the tower tonight, as Buck, the "Usurper," has taken it over.

---

### ANALYSIS

The first three episodes of *Ulysses* center upon Stephen Dedalus, Joyce's autobiographical protagonist from *A Portrait of the Artist as a Young Man.* We left Stephen at the end of *Portrait,* an ambitious and slightly arrogant young poet who was just finishing college and leaving Dublin for Paris in the Spring of 1902. *Ulysses* picks up just over two years later. In Paris, Stephen lived a bohemian-intellectual lifestyle after abandoning medical school. Stephen was called back from Paris by his mother's illness, probably in the summer of 1903. Almost a year later—June 16, 1904—we see Stephen in "Telemachus," unresigned to life in Ireland and still dressed in mourning for his mother. He is as yet unrealized as an artist.

The novel's epic *in medias res* ("in the middle of things") opening begins, however, not with Stephen, but with Buck Mulligan, who appears as a contrast to Stephen. Whereas Stephen is nearly silent and very reserved, Buck is boisterous and physically active. Buck and Stephen's relationship is fraught: Buck seeks to establish superiority over Stephen through mockery, yet he also trots out his cultural and intellectual knowledge to impress Stephen. Buck is associated with the consumption, recycling, and marketing of art, not the creation of it—he is likened to a medieval patron of arts and encourages Stephen to market his witticisms to Haines. Buck serves to reveal Stephen's stubborn pride. Buck's jokes that imply that Stephen is a servant, and Buck's eventual acquisition of the house key and Stephen's money lead to Stephen's final, frustrated thought of the chapter—"Usurper."

An early parallel between Stephen and Hamlet is set up in "Telemachus," through Stephen's brooding presence and the Elsinore-like setting of the Martello tower. In the context of this parallel, we can begin to understand Buck's joking references to Stephen's supposed madness and Stephen's resentment of Buck, the "Usurper," as related to Hamlet's seething, silent resentment of Claudius. However, no single parallel can be used to match a corresponding character in *Ulysses*. For example, while Hamlet is famously haunted by the death of his father, Stephen is haunted instead by the death of his mother. The complication of a direct relation between Stephen and Hamlet is also disturbed by the fact that Stephen himself is well aware of this relation—Buck informs us that Stephen has his own "Hamlet theory," which Haines mistakenly, though not insignificantly, thinks will connect the play to Stephen himself.

Episode One introduces us to Stephen's struggle with the ins and outs of Irish identity. The poet Yeats wrote "Who Goes with Fergus?," the poem that Buck sings, and that Stephen sang to his dying mother. Yeats is evoked in Episode One as a representative of the Irish Literary Revival, a movement of Irish writers contemporary with the setting of *Ulysses* who, in part, intended to define an insular sense of Irish identity, with the idea of making Ireland culturally, if not politically, independent from England. Stephen recognizes the milk woman as the type of earthy peasant figure that the Irish Literary Revivalists and other nationalists would idealize as a symbol of Ireland. Yet, for Stephen, the figure she represents is barren. Her submissiveness toward Buck and Haines confirms that she offers no release from Ireland's servitude. Additionally, the milk woman's failure to recognize the Irish that Haines speaks works to deflate such an idealized personification of national identity. Stephen, especially through his self-conscious pose as a continental bohemian, emerges in these opening chapters as a figure dismissive of this kind of insular Irish self-definition.

Haines's version of Irishness appears equally unacceptable. In light of his familiarity with Irish culture and history, Haines's passive and self-absolving "It seems history is to blame" seems particularly irresponsible and is met with disgust by Stephen. Stephen's remarks about his own servitude to England and Catholicism are meant to point out the power-relations that Haines attempts to complacently ignore. Stephen's addition of a third master—Ireland—is a somewhat proud attempt to set himself apart from the Irish masses, who take their own nationalism as a given. The theme of Stephen's perception of himself as a servant will persist throughout *Ulysses*. As in this discussion with Haines, fluctuations between perceptive recognition of and prideful resistence to various authorities define the progression of Stephen's day.

## EPISODE TWO: "NESTOR"

> Amor matris: *subjective and objective genitive.*
> (See QUOTATIONS, p. 82)

### SUMMARY

Stephen is teaching a history class on Pyrrhus's victory—the class is not very disciplined. He drills the students, and a boy named Armstrong phonetically guesses that Pyrrhus was "a pier." Stephen indulges him and expands on Armstrong's answer, calling a pier "a disappointed bridge." He imagines himself subserviently dropping this witticism later for Haines's amusement. Thinking of Phyrrus's and Caesar's murders, Stephen wonders about the philosophical inevitability of certain historical events—is history the fulfillment of the only possible course of events, or one of many?

Stephen takes the class through Milton's *Lycidas* as he continues to ponder his own questions about history, questions he thought about while reading Aristotle in a Paris library. An image from Milton's poem makes Stephen think of God's effect on all men. Stephen thinks of the lines of a common riddle then decides to tell the students his own riddle as they gather their things and prepare to leave to play field hockey. Stephen alone laughs at his impenetrable riddle about a fox burying his grandmother under a bush.

The students leave, except for Sargent, who needs help with his arithmatic. Stephen looks at the ugly Sargent and imagines Sargent's mother's love for him. Stephen shows Sargent the sums, thinking briefly of Buck's joke that Stephen's Hamlet theory is proven by algebra. Thinking again of *amor matris,* or mother's love, Stephen is reminded of himself as a child, clumsy like Sargent. Sargent heads outside to join the hockey game. Stephen walks outside, then goes to wait in Deasy's office while Deasy, the schoolmaster, settles a hockey dispute.

Mr. Deasy pays Stephen his wages and shows off his savings box. Deasy lectures Stephen on the satisfaction of money earned and the importance of keeping money carefully and of saving it. Deasy remarks that an Englishman's greatest pride is the ability to claim he has paid his own way and owes nothing. Stephen mentally tallies up his own abundant debts.

Deasy imagines that Stephen, whom he assumes is Fenian, or an Irish Catholic nationalist, disrespects Deasy as a Tory—a Protestant loyal to the English. Deasy argues his Irish credentials—he has witnessed much Irish history. Deasy then asks Stephen to use his influence to get a letter of Deasy's printed in the newspaper. While he finishes typing it, Stephen looks around his office at the portraits of racehorses and remembers a trip to the racetrack with his old friend Cranly.

Stephen hears shouts welcoming a goal scored on the hockey field. Deasy hands Stephen his completed letter and Stephen skims it. The letter warns of the dangers of foot-and-mouth cattle disease and suggests that it can be cured. It seems that Deasy resents the influence of those people who currently have power over the situation. He also seems to blame Jews for similar corruption and destruction of national economies. Stephen argues that greedy merchants can be Jewish or gentile, but Deasy insists that the Jews have sinned against "the light."

Stephen remembers the Jewish merchants standing outside the Paris stock exchange. Stephen again challenges Deasy, asking who has not sinned against the light. Stephen rejects Deasy's rendering of the past, and states, "History is a nightmare from which I am trying to awake." Ironically, a goal is scored outside in the hockey game as Deasy speaks of history as the movement toward the "goal" of God's manifestation. Stephen counters that God is no more than "a shout in the street." Deasy argues first that all have sinned, then blames woman for bringing sin into the world. He lists women of history who have caused destruction.

Deasy predicts that Stephen will not remain at the school long, because he is not a born teacher. Stephen suggests that he may be a learner rather than a teacher. Stephen signals the end of the discussion by returning to the subject of Deasy's letter. Stephen will try to get it published in two newspapers. Stephen walks out of the school, pondering his own subservience to Deasy. Deasy runs after him to make one last jab against the Jews—Ireland has never persecuted the Jews because they were never let in to the country.

## ANALYSIS

*History is a nightmare from which I am trying to awake.*
(See QUOTATIONS, p. 82)

Episode Two, "Nestor," takes place at the boys school where Stephen teaches. It is a half-day for the students and Stephen will leave for the day after he teaches his class and is paid by Mr. Deasy. The episode focuses on teaching and learning. We see Stephen positioned first as a teacher and then as a student in his conversation with Mr. Deasy. The subject of both educational scenes is history, and history as linked to memory. Stephen's history lesson for his class relies on their memory of learned historical facts. Mr. Deasy's impromptu history lesson for Stephen is anchored by Deasy's own personal memories of historical events. Stephen himself resists the linking of history with memory. For Deasy to define history in terms of his personal recollections affords him too much control over the reconstruction of it (thus do Haines and Deasy use history to absolve themselves of responsibility). For Stephen, history is something that he cannot control: "History is a nightmare from which I am trying to awake." Stephen's statement refers both to his grappling with the circumstances of his own past, and to the philosophical problem of how history should be used to understand present circumstances.

Part of Stephen's personal history that has nightmarishly, though subtly, plagued him through this episode and the first is his mother's death. Stephen's unsolvable riddle about the fox burying his grand-mother suggests this personal pain. As he tutors Sargent, Stephen's ruminations about a mother's love and love for one's mother also evoke her absence and stand in contrast to Deasy's later misogyny. Stephen's imagination of a mother's love creates a moment of compassion and allows for an effective teaching between Stephen and Sargent. Other-wise, Stephen's interactions with his students have been distracted and cryptic. Stephen himself credits Deasy with accuracy when Deasy intu-its later in the chapter that Stephen was not born to be a teacher.

On the whole, Deasy seems pompous and self-righteous. We are pre-pared for the didactic nature of Deasy's conversation with Stephen by our first glimpse of Deasy on the hockey field, yelling at the students without listening to them. Deasy is unperceptive—mistakenly assuming that Stephen is Fenian, he launches into a history lecture. The purpose of this lecture is less to teach than to assert authority, an authority that is undermined by several factual errors that Deasy makes. Like Haines, Deasy (a Unionist from the north) is pro-British as well as anti-Semitic. Just as Haines used history to clear himself of blame in Episode One ("It seems history is to blame"), so Deasy uses history to blame others, nota-bly Jews and women.

This prelude of anti-Semitism will be evoked later in the day, as Jew-ish Leopold Bloom faces similar bigotry. Deasy's anti-Semitism rests on his sense that the mercantile Jews have brought decay to England. According to Deasy, the Jews have sinned against "the light," the light being those Christians who understand history as moving toward one goal—the manifestation of God's plan. But the presentation of Deasy's character undermines his own convictions. Instead of Christianity and light, Deasy himself deals in coins and material goods. His moralistic color scheme, in which good Christians are light and dangerous Jews are dark, is not to be the color scheme of *Ulysses,* in which the two heroes, Stephen and Bloom, are dressed in black, and the dangerous characters, such as Buck Mulligan, are associated with brightness.

Notably, Stephen challenges only Deasy's anti-Semitism during the conversation, and not any other of Deasy's ill-considered comments. Stephen's overall passivity and politeness toward Deasy seem to have more to do with his unwillingness to participate in a political argument on Deasy's terms. Stephen's bohemian-intellectual comment that God is "a shout in the street" is a clear departure from the terms of Deasy's argument, and it confuses him. Deasy is aggressive and likens their conversation to armed confrontation—breaking lances. Stephen dislikes violence. The subject of his morning history lesson, Pyrrhus, is notable for winning a battle, yet reckoning the cost of the violence too great. During his conversation with Deasy, Stephen is rattled by the noises from the hockey field outside. He envisions the field hockey match as a joust and imagines the boys' moving bodies as sounds and gestures of bloody battle. Rather than remaining in this atmosphere, prey to Deasy's aggressive comments, Stephen politely signals the end of the conversation by rustling the sheets of Deasy's letter. When Deasy runs after Stephen in the driveway to report an anti-Semitic joke, Stephen's non-participation is palpable. His thoughts are silent; his mind has moved on.

## EPISODE THREE: "PROTEUS"

### SUMMARY

Stephen walks on the beach, contemplating the difference between the material world as it exists and as it is registered by his eyes. Stephen closes his eyes and lets his hearing take over—rhythms emerge.

Opening his eyes, Stephen notices two midwives, Mrs. Florence MacCabe and another woman. Stephen imagines that one has a miscarried fetus in her bag. He imagines an umbilical cord as a telephone line running back through history through which he could place a call to "Edenville." Stephen pictures Eve's navel-less stomach. He considers woman's original sin, and then his own conception. Stephen contrasts his own conception with that of Christ. According to the Nicene Creed, a part of the Catholic mass, Christ was "begotten, not made," meaning that he is part of the same essence as God the Father and was not made by God the Father out of nothing. Stephen, in contrast, was "made not begotten," in that though he has biological parents, his soul was created out of nothing and bears no relation to his father's. Stephen would like to argue the specifics of divine conception (are the Father and the Son the same being or not?) with heretic-scholars of the past.

The sea air blows upon him, and Stephen remembers that he must take Deasy's letter to the newspaper, then meet Buck at The Ship pub at

12:30. He considers turning off the beach to visit his aunt Sara. He imagines his father's mocking reaction to such a visit (his father is disgusted by his brother-in-law, Richie, who is Sara's husband). Stephen imagines the scene if he were to visit: Richie's son Walter would let him in and uncle Richie, who has back trouble, would greet Stephen from bed.

Coming out of his reverie, Stephen remembers feeling ashamed of his family when he was a child. This disgust for his family brings Jonathan Swift to mind—Swift's disgust for the masses is evidenced in his novel *Gulliver's Travels* by the noble Houyhnhnm horses and beastly Yahoo men. He thinks of Swift, with a priestly tonsured head, climbing a pole to escape the masses. Stephen thinks of priests all around the city and of the piety and intellectual pretensions of his youth.

Stephen notices he has passed the turnoff for Sara's. Heading toward the Pigeonhouse, Stephen thinks about pigeons: specifically, the Virgin Mary's insistence that her pregnancy was caused by a pigeon (as recorded in Léo Taxil's *La Vie de Jesus*). He thinks of Patrice Egan, the son of Kevin Egan, a "wild goose" (Irish nationalist in exile) whom Stephen knew in Paris. He remembers himself in Paris as a medical student with little money. He remembers arriving once at the post office too late to cash a money order from his mother. Stephen's ambitions for his life in Paris were suddenly halted by a telegram from his father, calling Stephen home to his mother's deathbed. He thinks back to Buck's aunt's insistence that Stephen killed his mother by refusing to pray at her deathbed.

Stephen remembers the sights and sounds of Paris, and of Kevin Egan's conversations about nationalism, strange French customs, and his Irish youth. Stephen walks to the edge of the sea and back, scanning the horizon for the Martello tower. He again vows not to sleep there tonight with Buck and Haines. He sits on a rock and notices the carcass of a dog. A live dog runs across the beach, back to two people. Stephen imagines the beach scene when the first Danish Vikings invaded Dublin.

The barking dog runs toward Stephen, and Stephen contemplates his fear of the dog. Considering various "Pretenders" to crowns in history, Stephen wonders if he, too, is a pretender. He notices that the two figures with the dog are a man and a woman, cocklepickers. He watches as the dog sniffs at the carcass and is scolded by his master. The dog pisses, then digs in the sand. Stephen remembers his morning riddle about the fox who buried his own grandmother.

Stephen tries to remember the dream he was having last night: a man holding a melon was leading Stephen on a red carpet. Watching the woman cocklepicker, Stephen is reminded of a past sexual encounter in Fumbally's lane. The couple pass Stephen, looking at his hat. Stephen constructs a poem in his head and jots it down on a scrap torn from Deasy's letter. Stephen wonders who the "she" of his poem would be. He longs for affection. Stephen lies back and contemplates his borrowed boots and small feet that once fit into a woman's shoes. He pisses. He thinks again of the drowned man's body. Stephen gets up to leave, picks his nose, then looks over his shoulder to see if anyone has seen. He sees a ship approaching.

---

ANALYSIS

There is very little action in Episode Three and only one line of dialogue—the chapter consists almost entirely of Stephen's thoughts. Joyce's scant use of punctuation makes it somewhat difficult in Episodes One and Two to distinguish between third-person narrative, interior monologue, and dialogue. In Episode Three, the problem becomes not how to distinguish Stephen's interior monologue from all else, but how to follow the twists and turns of that monologue itself. Stephen is an extremely educated young man—his thoughts therefore flit over a host of scholarly texts and several different languages. Episode Three also offers a compendium of the symbols we have seen thus far, as Stephen's mind works in the language of symbols from earlier in the morning. Thus Deasy's shell collection, the sea as mother from Episode One, and drowned male bodies recur in Episode Three and become motifs.

Thus far this morning, we have seen Stephen in his social and professional guises, with smatterings of his private thoughts. The more personal nature of Episode Three allows us to sense an undertone of suffering (expressed through the recurring themes of death, drowning, and decay) in Stephen's thoughts. The Stephen Dedalus from the end of *A Portrait of the Artist as a Young Man* was isolated and full of pride. He had ceased to communicate with those around him, and was cerebrally focused on his artistic coming-of-age and Parisian exile. The Stephen of *Ulysses* is chastened by his untriumphant return to Ireland, and has begun to learn the error of his ways—he must acknowledge and interact with the world around him if he ever wishes to mature as an artist. The beginnings of Stephen's maturation can be seen here in his willingness to be critical of his younger self.

At the beginning of the episode, Stephen briefly considers philosophical solipsism—the idea that the world only exists in our individual perceptions of it. He rehearses the refutation of this theory—knocking his walking-stick against a rock. Despite his practical refutation of solipsism, however, Stephen's attention in the first part of the episode is focused not on his surroundings, but on his thoughts and on his imaginative recreations of his surroundings. As the episode goes on, though, Stephen begins apprehending more and more of his physical surroundings—by the end of the chapter we finally have a sense, for the first time, of the presence of Stephen's body, as he urinates, touches his rotten teeth, picks his nose, and looks over his shoulder. His attentiveness to his own physical presence within his surroundings leads him to produce art. He uses the cocklepicker as concrete inspiration for a poem involving a female figure. Stephen's artistic maturation will not be accomplished today, June 16, 1904, but the direction in which Stephen must continue is laid out for us in Episode Three. Leopold Bloom, appearing finally in Episode Four, also serves as a model of outward attentiveness in opposition to the cerebral Stephen.

Episode Three is associated with Proteus, the shape-shifting god. Accordingly, the episode is full of transformations of all sorts—reincarnation, reproduction, mystical morphing, and material change. Stephen sees figures and landscapes around him and shape-shifts them in his poetic consciousness—for example, he associates the running dog with a bear, a fawn, a wolf, a calf, a panther, and a vulture. Transformation, in which one element translates into a new context (for example, a soul into a new body), also characterizes the movement of Stephen's thought. His associations and topic-jumps are not always logic-based. They often rely on one word or even the sound of a word to introduce an entirely new thought into his mind. For example, the dog's morphing into a panther brings to mind Haines's dream about a panther, which then causes Stephen to try to remember what he himself had been dreaming about when Haines's moaning woke him.

Thus far in *Ulysses,* we have seen Stephen to be concerned with mothers—for example, his own mother's death, the concept of maternal love, and Eve as the original mother. In Episode Three, we get Stephen's first thoughts about fathers, his own father specifically, from whom Stephen pointedly distances himself here. Kevin Egan, the exiled Irish nationalist, functions as a sort of father figure in Episode Three as well. To the extent that he is paternal, Egan represents the restrictive pull of fidelity to country and to God and to an idealized past—restrictions that Stephen would prefer to avoid. Stephen's actual lack of his mother and his willed lack of a father underlies the movement toward an expected climax in which Stephen might find surrogate parents in Leopold and Molly Bloom.

# EPISODE FOUR: "CALYPSO"

## SUMMARY
Leopold Bloom fixes breakfast for his wife, Molly, and feeds his cat. Bending down with his hands on his knees, he wonders what he looks like to the cat and how her whiskers work as she laps milk. Bloom considers what he will get from the butcher for his own breakfast. He creeps upstairs to ask Molly if she would like anything from outside. Molly mumbles no and the bed jingles under her. Bloom thinks about the bed, which Molly brought with her from Gibraltar, where she was raised by her father, Major Tweedy.

Bloom checks on a slip of paper in his hat and his lucky potato, and he makes a note to retrieve his house keys from upstairs before he leaves for the day. Bloom walks outside and anticipates being warm in the black clothes he will wear for Paddy Dignam's funeral today. He imagines walking a path around the middle part of the globe in front of the sun's path to remain the same age and he pictures the Eastern landscapes. But no, he reasons, his mental images are fictional material, not accurate. Bloom passes Larry O'Rourke's pub and wonders if he should stop and mention Dignam's funeral, but he simply wishes O'Rourke a good day instead. Blooms tries to figure how all the small-time pub owners like O'Rourke make money, given how many pubs there are in Dublin. Bloom passes a school and listens to the students recite their alphabet and Irish place names. Bloom imagines his own Irish place name, "Slieve Bloom."

Bloom arrives at Dlugacz's, the butcher shop. He sees one kidney left and hopes the woman in front of him does not buy it. Bloom picks up a sheet of the wrapping newspaper and reads the ads. The woman pays for her order, and Bloom points to the kidney, hoping to fill his order quickly so that he can follow her home and watch her hips move. Too late to catch her, he continues reading his sheet of newspaper on the way home. It advertises fruit plantations for speculation in Palestine and Bloom thinks of fruits from the Mediterranean and Middle East. Bloom passes a man he knows who does not see him.

As a cloud passes over the sun, Bloom's thoughts turn sour with a more barren vision of the Middle East and the tragedy of the Jewish race. Bloom vows to improve his mood by beginning his morning exercises again, then turns his attention to an unrented piece of real estate on his street and finally to Molly. The sun comes back out and a blond girl runs past Bloom.

Bloom finds two letters and a card in the hall. Bloom senses that the one for Molly is from Blazes Boylan, Molly's associate and possible lover. Entering the bedroom, he gives Molly the letter and a card from their daughter Milly in Mullingar. Molly puts Boylan's letter under her pillow and reads Milly's card. Bloom goes downstairs to prepare the tea and kidney. He skims his own letter from Milly.

Bloom brings Molly her breakfast in bed. Bloom asks her about her letter, and she explains that Boylan is bringing over the concert program this afternoon. Molly will sing *"Là ci darem"* and "Love's Old Sweet Song." Molly directs Bloom to bring her a book. While he retrieves the book, Bloom rehearses lines from *"Là ci darem"* in his head, wondering if Molly will pronounce them correctly. Molly takes the book, a racy novel entitled *Ruby: the Pride of the Ring*, and finds the word she wanted to ask Bloom about—"metempsychosis." Bloom rehearses the etymology, but Molly asks for the meaning in plain terms. Bloom explains reincarnation. Spotting a painting of a nymph over their bed, he gives her the example of nymphs returning in another form, such as a tree. Molly asks for another book by Paul de Kock.

Molly smells Bloom's kidney burning and he runs downstairs to save it. Bloom sits down to eat and rereads Milly's letter. She thanks him for her birthday present and mentions a boyfriend, Bannon. Bloom thinks of Milly's childhood and of his son Rudy, who died several days after birth. He thinks about Milly becoming a woman and being aware of her own attractiveness. Since Milly has mentioned Boylan in her letter, he thinks of Blazes Boylan's confidence and feels helpless and regretful. He thinks of visiting Milly.

Bloom fetches a copy of the magazine *Titbits* and heads toward the outhouse to relieve himself. Bloom thinks of plans for his garden. On the toilet, Bloom reads the story *Matcham's Masterstroke* by Philip Beaufoy. Satisfied with the regularity of his bowel movement, he finishes the story and thinks he could write a story and be paid for it. He could write about a proverb or about Molly's chatter. Bloom wipes himself with part of the story. He reminds himself to check the funeral time in the paper. Hearing the church bells, he thinks with pity about Dignam.

---

## ANALYSIS

Episodes One, Two, and Three constituted a prologue centering on Stephen as a Telemachus figure. With Episode Four, the morning begins again—it is 8:00 A.M., and this chapter takes place simultaneously to Episode One as we begin the adventures of "Odysseus," Leopold Bloom. Joyce subtly emphasizes this simultaneity by having both Stephen and Bloom notice the same cloud move briefly over the sun. Thematic correspondences also emphasize the simultaneity: both Stephen and Bloom prepare breakfast for others; both are dressed in mourning; both are dispossessed of their homes (Buck takes charge of the tower, Molly and Boylan will take over the Bloom house); both leave without their house keys.

Aside from these thematic correspondences, Episode Four also serves to set up differences between Bloom and Stephen. Whereas Stephen resentfully helped serve breakfast to Haines in Episode One, Bloom solicitously prepares his wife's and his cat's breakfasts before his own. The movements of Bloom's body are foregrounded while Stephen's body was virtually absent from Episode One's narrative. Finally, Stephen's last word in Episode One—"Usurper"—was theatrically bitter, while Bloom's last line in Episode Four—"Poor Dignam!"—is sympathetic and mundane.

The character differences between Bloom and Stephen are most clearly evident in their respective thought processes. As we see in Episode Three, a concrete thing turns into an abstract thought in Stephen's consciousness, and these abstractions often lead back to Stephen himself. Bloom, however, perceives details by putting them in a larger context outside himself. Thus when Bloom walks past Larry O'Rourke's pub, the establishment spurs thoughts of comparative establishments and of the larger trend of small-time pubowners in Dublin. Whereas Stephen's trains of thought take him further and further from reality, Bloom checks himself when his imaginings become unrealistic, as with his colorful mental image of walking around the globe. When the cloud passes over the sun in Episode One, Stephen quickly descends into depressive thoughts and is only (partly) revived by the intervention of Buck. Bloom's thoughts also turn depressingly to death when the same cloud passes over the sun on his way back from the butcher's, yet Bloom pragmatically and deliberately revives his optimism. Finally, whereas Stephen's thought processes focus on philosophical or aesthetic problems and terms, Bloom's mind is practically curious and he answers his questions with practical experience and science.

Bloom begins his daily wanderings with his trip to the butcher's. Bloom's wandering sets him in relation to both Odysseus and the tropic figure of the Wandering Jew. Bloom's attitude toward Judaism, however, is presented as ambivalent at best. He shows practical and romantic interest in the movement for a Jewish homeland and in the newspaper ads for start-up plantations in Palestine. Yet he purposely does not return a glance of implied solidarity from the Jewish butcher and he does not follow Jewish dietary restrictions. The nature of Bloom's Judaism is not fully revealed in *Ulysses*—instead, Joyce shows that judgments about Bloom's Judaism reveal more about the other characters than they reveal about Bloom himself. Bloom is also clearly aligned with Irish identity through various details in Episode Four, such as his Irish-language personal place name, "Slieve Bloom," and his potato talisman.

Bloom is somewhat feminized in Episode Four through the reversal of household roles—Molly remains in bed and orders Bloom to get her breakfast, tea, and a novel. He suspects at some level that his wife—a concert soprano—is, or will be, conducting an affair with her concert manager, Hugh "Blazes" Boylan. But Bloom's thoughts reflect his feeling of powerlessness to stop his afternoon visit, and in a larger sense to stop the infidelity of his wife or the impending sexual activity of his fifteen-year-old daughter, Milly. As Odysseus was helplessly enthralled to Calypso in *The Odyssey*, so is Bloom presented in "Calypso" as paralyzed and enamored by Molly. Thus we see Joyce using the Homeric parallels to produce irony—Molly here is the enchanting Calypso and later the dutiful Penelope. Similarly, Bloom is Odysseus, yet we discover in Episode Four that his only son, Rudy, died soon after birth.

# EPISODE FIVE: "THE LOTUS EATERS"

## SUMMARY

Bloom walks a roundabout route toward the downtown post office, thinking about the people he passes and about the funeral he will attend at 11:00 A.M. While reading packet labels in the window of the Belfast and Oriental Tea Company, Bloom takes out the postal card for his pseudo-nym, Henry Flower. Inspired by the tea labels, Bloom imagines the heady atmosphere of the East. He surreptitiously walks into the post office and picks up a typed letter addressed to his pseudonym.

Outside the post office, Bloom opens his letter, but before he can read it, he is accosted by McCoy. Bloom makes small talk with McCoy while he tries to determine what is pinned to the letter, now in his pocket. While Bloom watches a sexy, upper-class woman across the street, McCoy makes small talk about Paddy Dignam's death, which he heard about from Bantam Lyons. Bloom anticipates seeing the woman's leg as she steps into her cab, but a tram blocks his view. Still chatting with McCoy, Bloom opens his newspaper and reads an ad: *"What is a home without / Plumtree's Potted Meat? / Incomplete. / With it an abode of bliss."* McCoy and Bloom speak about Molly's upcoming concert tour (McCoy's wife is an aspiring singer). Bloom thinks of Boylan's letter this morning and skirts the topic of Boylan's management of Molly's tour. Taking leave of Bloom, McCoy asks him to put McCoy's name down in the Dignam's funeral register. As McCoy leaves, Bloom thinks of the inferior singing ability of McCoy's wife.

Bloom sees an advertisement for the play *Leah*. Bloom remembers the story line, which involves the blind, dying Abraham recognizing the voice of his long-lost son, Nathan. This reminds Bloom of his own father's death. Bloom finally pulls out his letter—it has a flower inside. The letter is from his erotic penpal, Martha Clifford. In it, she asks to meet her correspondent in person, calls him "naughty" for using a certain word in his last letter, and, finally, asks him what kind of perfume his wife uses. Bloom puts the letter back in his pocket. He will never agree to meet her, but he will push further with the wording of his next letter. Bloom pulls the flower pin out of the enclosed flower and contemplates the many pins of women's clothes. A song comes to mind: "O, Mairy lost the pin of her drawers. . . ." He thinks of the names Martha and Mary, and of a painting of the biblical Martha and Mary.

Under a railway arch, Bloom tears up the envelope from Martha. Bloom steps into the backdoor of a church, reads the missionary notice, and ponders tactics for bringing religion to natives. Inside the church, a ceremony is in progress. Bloom considers that churches provide opportunities for sitting close to attractive women. He thinks of the power of

Latin to stupefy. Sitting down in a pew, Bloom ponders the communal feeling that must come from taking communion.

He thinks about Martha acting indignantly respectable one minute about his diction, but asking to meet with him (a married man) the next minute. This discrepancy reminds Bloom of the turncoat Carey, who had a respectable, religious life, but was also involved with the "Invincibles" who committed the Phoenix Park murders. Bloom watches the priest rinse out the wine chalice and wonders why they do not use Guinness or another beverage. Looking at the choir loft, Bloom thinks of Molly's performance of the *Stabat Mater*. As the priest finishes the ceremony, Bloom admires the effectiveness of the institution of confession and the idea of reform. The mass ended, Bloom gets up to leave before donations are requested. Bloom checks the time and heads toward Sweny's to order Molly's lotion, though he has left the recipe (along with his key) at home in his regular trousers.

At the chemist's, Bloom thinks of alchemy and sedatives. While the chemist searches for the lotion recipe, Bloom thinks of Molly's lovely skin and wonders if he has time for a bath. Bloom takes a lemon soap from the chemist and plans to return later to pick up the lotion and pay for both. As he leaves the shop, Bloom runs into Bantam Lyons. Lyons asks to see Bloom's newspaper so he can check on a horse race. Bloom tells Lyons he can keep the paper since Bloom was only going to throw it away. Lyons, mistaking Bloom's statement for a tip on a racehorse, hands the paper back to Bloom, thanks him and rushes off. Bloom thinks disgustedly about betting fever and begins to walk toward the public baths. He critiques an ineffective advertisement for college sports. He greets Hornblower, the porter, and thinks ahead to the moment when his body will be naked and reclined in a tub, his penis limp and floating like a flower.

---

## ANALYSIS

Episode Five, "The Lotus Eaters," is the first episode in which the thematic parallel to Homer begins to dominate the text. In *The Odyssey*, Odysseus's men eat the flower of the Lotus Eaters and become drowsily complacent, forgetting about their quest to return home. In Episode Five, it is mid-morning and Bloom's thoughts are lazy as he digests his breakfast and kills time before Paddy Dignam's funeral at 11:00. Bloom's attention wanders, yet the motif tying together many of his sentiments and observations is intoxication or drugged escapism. We are prepared for the motif from the opening page of the episode— Bloom imagines the Far East as a lazily intoxicating place. This motif then extends to other scenarios: Bloom notices the stupefied, effete horses drawing a tram; he thinks of the calming narcotic effect of smoking. Bloom spends a large section of the episode considering the stupefying power of religious ceremony—he assumes that religious missionaries have to compete with a lazy, narcotic lifestyle to win over a native population, and he appreciates the stupefying effect of Latin. The motif of intoxicated escapism sets the appropriate mood for an episode in which not much happens, and Bloom is largely alone. The motif also points to Bloom's efforts to escape his own thoughts about Molly's impending infidelity.

Indeed, the motif of lazy intoxication leads to a set of related motifs, most of which point implicitly back to Molly. Bloom associates exotic narcotics with the East, and his imaginations of the East, in turn, relate to Molly. We learned in Episode Four that Molly grew up in Gibraltar, where her father, Major Tweedy, was stationed. In Bloom's mind, Molly's childhood in Gibraltar links up with thoughts about Turkey and the Crimean War, with thoughts about model farms and land schemes in Palestine, and, here in Episode Five, with imaginings of the lands and people even farther east in Ceylon or China. Because Bloom's varied mental pictures of the East connect with his sense of Molly's exoticism and eroticism, Molly remains present even in an episode devoted to Bloom's erotic correspondence with another woman—Martha Clifford.

Bloom's covert correspondence with Martha Clifford offers us another perspective on the Blooms' marriage. Instead of Molly being the adulterous one and Bloom the adoring husband, we begin to consider Bloom's own part in the lapse of their relations. Yet Bloom seems more temporarily amused by Martha's letter (spelling errors and all) than committed to having an affair with her. Our new perspective of Bloom in this episode also offers us glimpses of his more perverse tendencies: a desire to be punished, a fetish for women's underclothing, his fantasies about meeting a woman during or after church.

The scenario of the Martha-Bloom correspondence offers another motif related to the drugged escapism of the Lotus flower eaters—the motif of flowers themselves. Bloom chooses the pseudonym "Henry Flower" (a kind of synonym for "Bloom"). Martha encloses a yellow flower in her letter to Bloom. Yet even this motif leads back to Molly. Martha's flower has no scent, and the final question of her letter is about his wife's perfume. Accordingly, Bloom's imagination of a tryst with Martha segues through a dream of two biblical doting women, Mary and Martha, thus leading back to Molly, whose Christian name is Marion (Mary).

# Episode Six: "Hades"

## Summary

Bloom steps into a carriage after Martin Cunningham, Jack Power, and Simon Dedalus—they are going to Dignam's funeral. As the carriage begins to move, Bloom points out Stephen on the street. Simon disapprovingly asks if Mulligan is with him. Bloom thinks Simon is too vehement, but reasons that Simon is right to look out for Stephen, as Bloom would have for Rudy, if he had lived.

Cunningham starts to describe his night at the pub and then asks Dedalus if he has read Dan Dawson's speech in this morning's paper. Bloom moves to take out the paper for Dedalus, but Dedalus signals that it would be inappropriate to read it now. Bloom skims the obituaries and checks that he still has Martha's letter. Bloom's thoughts soon wander to Boylan and his upcoming afternoon visit. At this moment, the carriage passes Boylan in the street, and the other men salute him from the carriage. Bloom is flustered by the coincidence. He does not understand what Molly and the others see in Boylan. Power asks Bloom about Molly's concert, referring to her as *Madame,* which makes Bloom uncomfortable.

The carriage passes Reuben J. Dodd, a moneylender, and the men curse him. Cunningham remarks that they have all owed money to Dodd—except Bloom, his look implies. Bloom begins to tell a humorous story about how Dodd's son almost drowned, but Cunningham rudely takes over. The men soon check their laughter and reminisce sadly about Dignam. Bloom remarks that he died the best way, quickly and painlessly, but the other men disagree silently—Catholics fear a sudden death because one has no chance to repent. Power pronounces that the worst death is a suicide and Dedalus agrees. Cunningham, knowing that Bloom's father committed suicide, argues for a charitable attitude toward it. Bloom is appreciative of Cunningham's sympathy.

The carriage stops for a cattle crossing. Bloom wonders aloud why there is no tramline for the cattle and Cunningham agrees. Bloom also suggests funeral trams, but the others agree only reluctantly. Cunningham reasons that a tram would prevent hearse accidents, such as the one recently that ended with a coffin dumped onto the road. Bloom envisions Dignam spilling out of his coffin. The carriage passes a water canal that runs to Mullingar, where Milly lives, and Bloom considers visiting her. Meanwhile, Power points out the house where the Childs fratricide, a well-known murder, took place.

The carriage arrives and the men get out. Trailing behind, Cunningham fills Power in about Bloom's father's suicide. Bloom asks Tom Kernan if Dignam was insured. Ned Lambert reports that Cunningham is taking up a collection for the Dignam children. Bloom looks on

one of Dignam's sons with pity. They enter the church and kneel—
Bloom last. Bloom watches the unfamiliar ceremony and thinks about
the repetitiveness of a priest's job. The ceremony ends and the coffin is
carried outside.

As the procession passes May Dedalus's grave, Dedalus begins cry-
ing. Bloom thinks about the realities of death—specifically, the failure
of body organs. Corny Kelleher, the undertaker, joins them. Ahead,
John Henry Menton asks who Bloom is. Lambert explains that he is
Molly's husband. Menton fondly recalls dancing with Molly once, and
he harshly wonders why Molly married Bloom.

The cemetery caretaker, John O'Connell, approaches the men and
tells a good-natured joke. Bloom wonders what it would be like to be
O'Connell's wife—would the graveyard be distracting? He admires the
neatness of O'Connell's cemetery, but he thinks it would more efficient
to bury bodies vertically. He thinks about the fertilizing power of dead
bodies and imagines a system by which people would donate their bodies to fertilize gardens. Thinking of O'Connell's jokes, Bloom recalls the
joking grave diggers in *Hamlet*. However, Bloom thinks, one should not
joke about the dead during the two-year mourning period. In the back-
ground, O'Connell and Kelleher confer about tomorrow's funerals.

The men assemble around the grave, and Bloom wonders who the
man in the macintosh is—he is the unlucky thirteenth member of the
party, and he was not in the chapel for the service. Bloom thinks of his
own funeral plot with his mother and son in it already. He thinks of
the horror of being buried alive and how telephones in coffins would
prevent it.

The reporter, Hynes, asks Bloom for his full name. Bloom asks him
to mention McCoy's name, as well, as McCoy had requested in Episode
Five. He asks Bloom for the name of the unfamiliar man in the macintosh, but Bloom does not know it. Bloom watches as the grave diggers
finish. Bloom strolls through the cemetery, thinking that the money
spent on luxurious graves could be given to charities for the living and
that gravestones would be more interesting if they explained who the
person was. He thinks of his upcoming visit to his father's grave. He sees
a rat and thinks of a rat eating a corpse. Bloom is happy to be leaving the
cemetery, since he has been thinking about necrophilia, ghosts, hell, and
how a graveyard visit makes one feel closer to death. He passes Menton
on the way out and tells him his hat has a ding in it. Menton snubs him.

---

## ANALYSIS

Much of Episode Six is concerned with Bloom's relative isolation within
a social group. Bloom is positioned as a latecomer, an outsider, and an
anomaly in the cab with Dedalus, Cunningham, and Power; in the
chapel service; and in the cemetery in relation to Menton and other

attendees of Dignam's funeral. Bloom's exclusion is vaguely implicit: Bloom is invited to step in the cab last, and he is not referred to by his Christian name. He is not bantered with, and Hynes (to whom Bloom has lent money) admits to not knowing his Christian name. It is not clear how much Bloom recognizes his own exclusion. For example, the third-person narrator characterizes Cunningham as rude when he interrupts Bloom, yet Bloom himself thinks minutes later about Cunningham's capacity for sympathy. Aside from the imperious John Henry Menton, the other men's exclusion of Bloom does not take a vicious form—he is merely not as close to the men as they are to each other and is treated accordingly.

The men's attitude toward Bloom seems pointed only when it is implicitly connected to his Jewishness or to Molly. When the other men spot Reuben J. Dodd, their animosity for him as a moneylender merges with their anti-Semitism, and Bloom is implicitly excluded from their sentiments, both because of his Jewishness and because he has never had to borrow money. Bloom again feels vaguely attacked when Power, seeing Boylan, asks Bloom if he will be accompanying Molly and Boylan to the concert in Belfast and refers to Molly, less than respectfully, as *Madame.*

Bloom's thoughts in Episode Six do not focus on this social exclusion. Instead, Episode Six parallels Episode Three's thematic focus on fathers and sons. In Episode Three, we saw Stephen thinking for the first time about his father, Simon Dedalus, and about fathers in general, rather than solely about his dead mother. Here in Episode Six, we not only see Simon's view of his son Stephen, but we also see Bloom's thoughts move away from Molly and Milly to center on memories of his dead father and son and to thoughts about paternity generally. Here we learn explicitly that Bloom's father committed suicide several years ago, and Bloom's thoughts about him dovetail with thoughts about his son, Rudy, who died several days after birth. Bloom's thoughts on paternity extend easily in this episode from the personal to the general—he views other fathers and sons, such as Simon Dedalus and Dignam's young son, with an eye of understanding and sympathy. While Stephen, in Episode Three, seem to willfully isolate himself from his father, Bloom here suffers from his own father-son isolation—he has no means by which to continue his family line. Without a patriarchal history or future—the foundation of epics like *The Odyssey*—Bloom seems remarkably vulnerable in Episode Six.

The true pathos of Episode Six is not reserved for the funeral service, during which Bloom's thoughts seem humorously detached, giving us a defamiliarized version of the Catholic priest's activities. It is in this sense that *Ulysses* strives to be a truly realistic novel. Instead of depicting Bloom at the funeral as a character who feels as one is *supposed* to feel—awed, sentimental, or quietly sad—Joyce purports to show Bloom as he would *actually* feel, in all its messiness, self-centeredness, and inappropriateness. The pathos of "Hades," then, is reserved for unspectacular moments, or even repressed moments, such as Bloom's quietly panicked reaction when the men see and salute Blazes Boylan in the street. Bloom's reflexive and thorough study of his fingernails in response to Boylan's appearance is a restrained and implicit representation of pathos that makes a stronger bid for our sympathy than, for example, Simon Dedalus's scripted tearfulness near the grave of his wife, later in the episode.

## EPISODE SEVEN: "AEOLUS"

SUMMARY & ANALYSIS

### SUMMARY
Episode Seven takes place in the *Freeman* newspaper offices. Newspaper-like headlines break the episode up into smaller passages. Without the headlines, the episode reads much the same as previous episodes have.

In Dublin's city-center, tramcars, postal carts, and porter barrels simultaneously roll to their destinations. Bloom is in the back office of the *Freeman* getting a copy of his Keyes advertisement. Bloom walks through the printing rooms to the *Telegraph* offices, which are under the same ownership as the *Freeman*. He approaches the foreman, City Councillor Nanetti, who is Italian by birth and Irish by choice. Nanetti is speaking to Hynes about his report of Dignam's funeral. Hynes owes Bloom three shillings, and Bloom tries to tactfully remind him about it, but Hynes does not catch on.

Over the noise of the presses, Bloom describes the new design for the Keyes ad: two keys crossed, to evoke the independent parliament of the Isle of Man and thus the dream of Irish home-rule. Nanetti tells Bloom to get a copy of the design and to secure three months advertisement from Keyes. Bloom listens for a moment to the sound of papers shuffling through the printer, then walks toward the staff offices. Bloom watches the men typeset backward and thinks of his father reading Hebrew, from right to left. Bloom enters the *Evening Telegraph* office, where Professor MacHugh and Simon Dedalus are listening to Ned Lambert, who is mocking Dan Dawson's overwrought patriotic speech, reprinted in the morning newspaper. J.J. O'Molloy enters and the doorknob bumps Bloom. Bloom remembers O'Molloy's past as a promising lawyer—O'Molloy now has money troubles.

Lambert continues to mock Dawson's speech—Bloom agrees with the criticism but reminds himself that such speeches are well-received in person. Crawford enters, greeting MacHugh with mock disgust. Dedalus and Lambert leave for a drink. Bloom uses Crawford's telephone to call Keyes. Lenehan enters with the sports edition and proclaims that Sceptre will win today's horserace. We hear Bloom on the phone—he seems to have missed Keyes at his office. Re-entering the room, Bloom bumps into Lenehan. Bloom tells Crawford that he is headed out to set-tle the Keyes ad—Crawford could not care less. A minute later, MacHugh notices from the window that the newsboys are following Bloom, mimicking his jerky walk. Lenehan imitates it too.

O'Molloy offers MacHugh a cigarette. Lenehan lights their ciga-rettes, waiting to be offered one. Crawford jokes with MacHugh, a Latin professor, about the Roman Empire. Lenehan tries to tell a riddle, but no one listens.

O'Madden Burke enters with Stephen Dedalus behind him. Stephen hands Deasy's letter to Crawford. Crawford knows Deasy and com-ments on Deasy's ornery late wife, which helps Stephen understand Deasy's view that women are responsible for the sin of the world. Crawford skims Deasy's letter and agrees to publish it. MacHugh is arguing that the Greeks and the Irish are similar because they are dom-inated by other cultures (Roman and British, respectively) yet retain a spirituality that those cultures do not have. Lenehan finally tells his riddle. Crawford comments on the gathering of many talents in the room (literature, law, etc.). MacHugh remarks that Bloom would rep-resent the art of advertising, and O'Madden Burke adds that Mrs. Bloom would add vocal talent. Lenehan makes a suggestive comment about Molly.

Crawford asks Stephen to write something sharp for the paper. Crawford recalls the great talent of Ignatius Gallaher, who reported on the 1882 Phoenix Park murders (the British chief secretary and under-secretary were killed). This recollection sparks many individual stories about the murders and the Invincibles, the group who claimed respon-sibility. Some of them were hanged, but others remain alive, such as Skin-the-Goat, a character who will appear later in *Ulysses*. Mean-while, MacHugh answers the telephone. It is Bloom, but Crawford is too preoccupied with the conversation to speak with him.

O'Molloy tells Stephen that he and Professor Magennis were speak-ing of Stephen. They are curious about Stephen's opinion of A.E., the mystical poet. Stephen resists the urge to ask what Magennis said about him. MacHugh interrupts to describe the finest example of eloquence— John F. Taylor's speech at the Trinity College historical society debate over the revival of the Irish tongue. MacHugh re-enacts the speech, which equated the British, who threaten to culturally overwhelm the Irish, to the Egyptians, who threaten to completely assimilate the Jews.

Stephen suggests they adjourn to a pub, and Lenehan leads the way. O'Molloy holds Crawford behind to ask him for a loan. Stephen walks outside with Professor MacHugh and tells MacHugh a cryptic parable of two old virgins who go to the top of Nelson's pillar to see the views of Dublin and eat plums.

While Stephen tells his story, Crawford finally emerges outside and Bloom, on his way in, attempts to accost him on the front steps. Bloom wants approval for two month's renewal of the Keyes ad instead of three. Crawford turns this offer down flippantly and returns to his conversation with O'Molloy. He cannot lend O'Molloy any money.

Ahead, Stephen's story continues: the women, giddy at the top of the pillar, eat their plums and spit the seeds over the side. Stephen laughs— the story is apparently over, but the listeners are confused. Stephen names his story "A Pisgah Sight of Palestine" or "The Parable of the Plums." MacHugh laughs knowingly. Meanwhile, the trams and other vehicles all across the city continue to roll.

---

### ANALYSIS

Episode Seven, "Aeolus," is the first episode in which the text seems conscious of itself as a text. The newspaper-like headlines break up the otherwise-familiar text and suggest to the reader that an outside editor, author, or arranger is responsible for them. We are no longer involved in a one-on-one relation with the plot of *Ulysses*—someone is filtering this information for us.

The episode parallels the aftermath of Odysseus's visit to Aeolus, the god of the winds in the *Odyssey*. One of Odysseus's men disobeys him, opening a bag of winds that then blows them off-course. In the "Aeolus" episode of *Ulysses,* wind is represented by the windy rhetoric used in journalism and oratory. The newspaper-room setting of the chapter, the episode's headlines, and the men's own inflated speech, together with the conversation about rhetorical and journalistic triumphs, all support the theme of the episode. Additionally, within the headlines and within the general text of the episode, over sixty different rhetorical figures (such as hyperbole, metonymy, chiasmus) are demonstrated.

Episode Seven also recalls one of Joyce's earlier works—the short-story collection, *Dubliners*. Several *Dubliners* characters appear here (Lenehan, Ignatius Gallaher), and the sense of futility and paralysis of *Dubliners* filters into this episode depicting mid-day idleness, disappointment, and frustration. Just as Odysseus's ship was blown off-course by the winds released from the bag, several characters are thwarted in their individual quests. Bloom does not get the Keyes ad in the paper, O'Molloy does not get a loan from Crawford, Stephen never makes it to meet Buck at the Ship pub at noon. If rhetoric is a means for making arguments and convincing listeners, it gets short shrift here. Few comprehensive connections are made in this episode—points and arguments trail off or are swallowed in the noise of the newspaper pressrooms. Instead, language works to obscure and divide: inside jokes, cryptic remarks, and stage-whispered comments abound.

Episode Seven is the first episode in which Stephen and Bloom actually cross paths (at the very end of the episode). Notably, Stephen ignores Bloom, while Bloom, father-like, notes Stephen's newer boots and, with disapproval, that Stephen has muck on his shoes and is leading the way to the pub. Bloom's and Stephen's separate but equal time in the episode invites comparison between their appearances in the *Freeman* offices. Bloom fails in his task of securing the Keyes ad for three months, while Stephen succeeds in getting Deasy's letter printed. Stephen has the center of the room, physically and symbolically, while Bloom remains unseen on the outskirts, bumped more than once. Bloom is jokingly referred to as a representative for the art of advertising, while Stephen is treated like a near-equal by the men and is even offered the chance to write for the paper. We also notice the two men's differing approaches to the domain of public expression. Bloom, as we have seen, has a pragmatic approach to the art of writing, oratory, and advertising. In Episode Four, we saw him consider writing fiction himself, in part to make money by it. Stephen, though flattered by the newspapermen's high expectations for him, will not waste himself on their type of writing—he will remain focused on his art, his poetry.

# EPISODE EIGHT: "LESTRYGONIANS"

## SUMMARY

Bloom walks past a candy store. A man hands Bloom a throw-away flyer, advertising a visiting American evangelist. Bloom at first thinks his own name is on the flyer but then realizes it reads, "Blood of the Lamb."

Bloom passes Dilly Dedalus. Bloom pities the now motherless Dedaluses. Dilly looks thin, and Bloom thinks about the inhumanity of the Catholic Church, which forces parents to have more children than they can feed. Bloom walks over O'Connell bridge and tosses the throwaway over the side. He buys two Banbury cakes to feed the seagulls. He notices an advertisement on a rowboat in the harbor. He thinks about other effective places for ads, like placing a doctor's flyer about sexually transmitted diseases in a bathroom. Bloom suddenly wonders if Boylan has an STD.

Bloom thinks of an astronomy concept that he never fully understood—"parallax." Bloom remembers this morning's "metempsychosis" conversation. A line of men wearing advertising sandwich boards for Wisdom Hely's walk by. When Bloom worked at Hely's, his employers rejected his advertising idea of having women inside a transparent cart writing on Hely's stationary. Bloom tries to remember where he and Molly were living at that time.

Bloom runs into Josie Breen, whom he once courted. She is now married to Denis Breen, who is mentally off-balance. Mr. Breen received an anonymous postcard this morning, which cryptically read, "u.p.: up." Today, he is trying to take legal action against the joke. Bloom inquires after a mutual friend, Mina Purefoy, who has been in labor at the maternity hospital for three days. As Bloom and Mrs. Breen talk, another Dublin crazy man sashays by—Cashel Boyle O'Connor Fitzmaurice Tisdall Farrell.

Bloom continues on, past the *Irish Times* office—he remembers the newspaper ad he ran for a lady typist that attracted Martha. He had another application—Lizzie Twigg—but she offered A.E. as a reference and thus seemed too literary, possibly ugly. His thoughts switch to Mina Purefoy and her perpetual pregnancies.

Passing a group of policemen, Bloom remembers watching a mounted policemen chase down a group of medical students who were shouting anti-British sentiments. Bloom guesses those medical students are probably now part of the institutions they were criticizing. He thinks about other turncoats—Carey of the Invincibles and house servants who inform on their employers.

A cloud blocks the sun, and Bloom thinks gloomily that the cycles of life—Dignam's death, Mrs. Purefoy's birthing—are meaningless. A.E. and a young, sloppily dressed woman, possibly Lizzie Twigg herself, pass Bloom.

Passing an optician's shop, Bloom thinks again about parallax and eclipses. He experimentally holds up his little finger to blot out the sun. He remembers the night that he and Molly walked with Boylan under the moon—he wonders if Molly and Boylan were touching. Bloom passes Bob Doran, clearly on his annual drinking bender. Bloom thinks about how men rely on alcohol for social interaction.

Overwhelmed by hunger, Bloom enters the Burton restaurant. Bloom is immediately disgusted by the spectacle of many ill-mannered men eating. He leaves and heads toward Davy Byrne's for a light snack instead.

Bloom enters Davy Byrne's, and Nosey Flynn greets him from the corner. Flynn asks about Molly and her upcoming singing tour. Flynn mentions Boylan, and Bloom is unpleasantly reminded of Boylan's impending visit to Molly. Flynn discusses the Gold Cup horserace. Bloom eats and is silently critical of Flynn.

Bloom looks above the bar at the tins of food. He ruminates about food: odd types, poisonous berries, aphrodisiacs, quirky personal favorites. Bloom notices two flies stuck on the window pane. He warmly remembers an intimate moment with Molly on the hill on Howth: as Bloom lay on top of her, Molly fed him seedcake out of her mouth, and they made love. Looking back at the flies, Bloom thinks sadly of the disparity between himself then and now.

Staring at the pleasing wood bar, Bloom contemplates beauty. He equates beauty with untouchable goddesses, such as the statues in the National Museum. He wonders if there's anything under the statues' robes and vows to sneak a look later today. Bloom finishes his wine and heads to the outhouse.

Davy Byrne is curious about Bloom. Flynn begins gossiping: he reports on Bloom's career, his participation in the Freemasons, how rarely he is drunk, and his refusal to sign his name to any contracts. Paddy Leonard, Bantam Lyons, and Tom Rochford enter and order drinks. They discuss Lyons's Gold Cup race bet. Bloom walks back through the bar and out. Lyons whispers that Bloom gave him the tip.

Out on the street, Bloom remembers to head toward the National Library to look up the Keyes ad. Bloom escorts a blind man across an intersection. Bloom thinks of how the other senses of blind people are heightened, like touch. He wonders what it would be like to be blind.

Bloom suddenly spots Boylan across the street. Panicked, he ducks into the gates of the National Museum.

---

## ANALYSIS

Bloom is primarily alone in Episode Eight, "Lestrygonians." He does not have any errands to run yet; he is merely strolling the city street and looking for lunch. In Episode Four, we were first introduced to Bloom as a preparer and eater of food, and, most notably in the opening lines, a meat lover. Yet, now, outside his own home, the prospect of getting and eating food is more overwhelming and problematic. Episode Eight corresponds to Odysseus's visit to the island of cannibals in the *Odyssey*. Under this thematic menace, the meat-loving Bloom opts not to eat at the Burton, where men shove meat into their mouths, and heads instead to Davy Byrne's for a vegetarian lunch.

The episode opens outside a candy shop, and food pervades Bloom's thoughts and serves as a tie-in with many other disparate topics. Thoughts of food connect with thoughts of pregnant women, from Molly's hunger for certain foods while pregnant to Mina Purefoy, currently in labor with many other mouths to feed at home. Food connects with sex, in Bloom's memory of making love with Molly years ago on a hill as she fed him a seedcake out of her mouth, and in his thoughts of aphrodisiacal food. Food connects with politics as Bloom thinks of the lavish dinners used to make political converts and of the horror of eating in a communal society. Food connects with creativity as Bloom wonders if what A.E. and other poets eat effects their poetry. Finally, food ties into Bloom's conception of types of "home." Bloom repeats to himself the Plumtree's ad he saw this morning in Episode Six (*"What is a home without Plumtree's potted meat? Incomplete. With it an abode of bliss."*), thus connecting this sinister-sounding meat product with marital bliss.

Finally, food connects with religious sacrifice. Religious sacrifice is connected to Bloom being cast as a Christ figure in the first lines of the episode, in which Bloom mistakenly reads his own name in the words *blood of the lamb* on an evangelist throwaway. Through a chain of further associations, Bloom is presented as a Christ-like martyr. His humanitarian acts that frame Episode Eight reinforce this alignment— Bloom produces Banbury cakes to feed thankless seagulls, and he helps a blind man across an intersection. If Bloom is set up as the sacrifice in this cannibalistic chapter, we might say that he is sacrificed to other Dublin men. Beyond the menacing eaters of the Burton, the men at Davy Byrne's—first Nosey Flynn, then Bantam Lyons and company— exercise power over Bloom. Their gossipy dialogue eats up the narrative of Bloom's inner consciousness as he goes to the outhouse. Instead of following Bloom's thoughts, we are suddenly presented with others' thoughts *about* Bloom, many of which are fallacious.

Episode Eight contains Bloom's thoughts of the word *parallax*. Bloom has problems understanding this word, as Molly had problems with *metempsychosis* this morning. Parallax is an astronomical term that roughly refers to the way in which an object seems to be positioned differently when viewed from a different vantage point. Though Bloom does not quite understand this concept, it will continue to appear, and it offers a key to one of the ways in which *Ulysses* works. As the novel continues, our thoughts and opinions about events and people will become continually revised as we hear about the same events and people from a different character—thus *Ulysses* features three main characters instead of only one.

# EPISODE NINE: "SCYLLA AND CHARYBDIS"

## SUMMARY
In the National Library director's office, sometime after 1:00 P.M., Stephen casually presents his "Hamlet theory" to John Eglinton, a critic and essayist; A.E., a poet; and Lyster, a librarian and Quaker. Stephen contends that Shakespeare associated himself with Hamlet's father, not with Hamlet himself. When the episode opens, Stephen is impatient with the older men's repetition of unoriginal, received wisdom on Shakespeare. John Eglinton puts Stephen in his place by mockingly inquiring about his own literary accomplishments or lack thereof. From the corner, A.E. expresses disdain for Stephen's Hamlet theory, maintaining that biographical criticism is useless because one should focus only on the depth expressed by the art. Stephen responds to Eglinton's mockery of his youth, pointing out that Aristotle was once Plato's pupil. Stephen shows off his knowledge of the philosophers' work.

Mr. Best, the librarian, enters—he has been showing Douglas Hyde's *Lovesongs of Connacht* to Haines. A.E. expresses his preference for Hyde's pastoral poems. Stephen continues with his theory by sketching a scene from Shakespeare's London: Shakespeare walks along the river to his own performance of *Hamlet* where he plays not Hamlet but the ghost of Hamlet's father. Stephen contends that Hamlet thus corresponds to Shakespeare's dead son, Hamnet, and unfaithful Gertrude represents Shakespeare's adulterous wife, Ann Hathaway. A.E. reiterates that a critic should focus on the work itself, not the details of the poet's personal life, such as his drinking habits or his debts. Stephen recalls that he himself owes A.E. some money.

Eglinton argues that Ann Hathaway is historically unimportant, and he cites biographers who depict Shakespeare's early marriage to Ann Hathaway as a mistake—a mistake he rectified by going to London. Stephen counters that geniuses make no mistakes. Lyster reenters the room. Stephen, drawing on the plots and imagery of the early plays, demonstrates that the older Ann seduced young Shakespeare in Stratford.

A.E. gets up to leave—he is expected elsewhere. Eglinton inquires if he will be at Moore's (an Irish novelist) tonight—Buck and Haines will be there. Lyster mentions that A.E. is compiling a volume of the work of young Irish poets. Someone suggests that Moore is the man to write the Irish epic. Stephen is resentful not to be included in the poetry collection, nor in their social circle. He vows to remember the snub. Stephen thanks A.E. for taking a copy of Deasy's letter for publication.

Eglinton returns to the argument: he believes that Shakespeare is Hamlet himself, as Hamlet is such a personal character. Stephen argues that Shakespeare's genius was such that he could give life to many characters. Still focusing on Ann Hathaway's adultery, Stephen points out that Shakespeare's middle plays are dark tragedies. His later, lighter plays testify (through their young female characters) to the arrival of Shakespeare's granddaughter, who reconciled the rift with the grandmother.

Stephen makes another point: the ghost of Hamlet's father inexplicably knows the means of his own murder and of his wife's betrayal. Shakespeare has granted him this extraneous knowledge because the character is part of Shakespeare himself. Buck, who has been standing in the doorway, mockingly applauds Stephen. Buck approaches Stephen and produces a cryptic telegram that Stephen sent to him at the Ship instead of showing up himself. Buck playfully chides Stephen for standing him and Haines up.

A library attendant comes to the door and summons Lyster to help a patron (Bloom) find the *Kilkenny People*. Buck recognizes Bloom standing in the hall and explains that he just saw Bloom in the National

Museum eyeing the rear end of a goddess statue. Implying that Bloom is a homosexual, Buck teasingly warns Stephen to beware of Bloom.

Stephen continues: while Shakespeare was in London living the high life with many sexual partners, Ann cheated on him back in Stratford—this hypothesis would explain why there is no other mention of her in the plays. Shakespeare's will pointedly left her only his "second-best bed."

Eglinton suggests that Shakespeare's father corresponds to the ghost of Hamlet's father. Stephen forcefully denies this supposition, insisting that the ghost of Hamlet's father is not Shakespeare's father, but Shakespeare himself, who was old and greying at the time the play was written. Fathers, Stephen digresses, are inconsequential. Paternity is unprovable and therefore insubstantial—fathers are linked to their children only by a brief sexual act.

Stephen goes on to suggest that Ann cheated on Shakespeare with his brothers, Edmund and Richard, whose names appear in Shakespeare's plays as adulterous or usurping brothers. Eglinton asks Stephen if he believes his own theory, and Stephen says no. Eglinton asks why he should expect payment for it if he does not believe it.

Buck tells Stephen it is time for a drink and they leave. Buck makes fun of Eglinton, a lonely bachelor. Buck reads aloud a play he was scribbling while Stephen argued—it is a farce, entitled *Everyman His Own Wife or A Honeymoon in the Hand*. As they walk out the front door, Stephen senses someone behind him—it is Bloom. Stephen steps away from Buck, and Bloom passes between them down the steps. Whispering, Buck again alludes jokingly to Bloom's lusty homosexuality. Stephen walks down the steps, feeling spent.

### ANALYSIS

In Episode Nine of *Ulysses,* we meet up again with Stephen, whom we last saw headed to a pub with the men from the *Freeman* office. He never met Haines and Buck at the Ship pub at 12:30, as they had arranged this morning. Instead, Stephen has wound up here, at the National Library, performing his "Hamlet theory." Stephen is trying to interest Eglinton and A.E. in publishing the theory, and in his own talent in general. Stephen's presentation is hardly formal—it rather takes the shape of a discussion between men-of-letters. There are frequent interruptions and digressions, and Stephen often ad-libs, using thoughts or the words of others from earlier in the day.

Episode Nine corresponds to Odysseus's trial-by-sea in which he must sail between Scylla, the six-headed monster situated on a rock, and Charybdis, a deadly whirlpool. The concept of negotiating two extremes plays out several times within the episode, most notably in the Plato-Aristotle dichotomy that Stephen mentions. Like Odysseus, Stephen sails closer to Scylla, and thus Stephen's thoughts and theories owe more to Aristotle's grounded, material, logical sense of the world (symbolized by the rock) than to Plato's sense of unembodied concepts or ideals (symbolized by the whirlpool).

This alignment explains why Stephen grounds Shakespeare's work in the lived reality of Shakespeare's life, whereas A.E. separates the man from the eternal ideas expressed in his work. Like Odysseus, Stephen cannot sail too close to Scylla's rock, though, and the threat of extreme materialism is represented by Buck and his physically based humor. Stephen also has to negotiate between his desire for acceptance from literary men such as Eglinton and A.E. and his disdain for such men and their movement, the Irish Literary Revival. Stephen is scornful of A.E.'s mysticism and Eglinton's superiority, but he is also bitterly sad at not being considered for A.E.'s compilation of young Irish poets or for the gathering at Moore's house.

Part of the reason that Eglinton and the others seem resistant to Stephen's Hamlet theory is that the theory is less a traditional piece of literary-critical investigation than an imaginative performance of one poet understanding another poet. We have seen Stephen, in the first three episodes of *Ulysses,* struggling with the circumstances of his own life and history and trying to understand how he can either incorporate them or overcome them to create art. Stephen's theory of Hamlet shows that Shakespeare often wrote his life and times into his work (the culmination being *Hamlet* as an expression of his bitterness at his wife's infidelity) and thus presents examples of how masterpieces can still be tied to the realities of lived experience.

Stephen's meditations on paternity take on a particular urgency in Episode Nine. Stephen envisions ideal paternity as literary creation—he argues that Shakespeare is not merely father to his son Hamnet but to all humanity. Stephen's further arguments about the tenuosity of the father-son relationship and the insignificance of fathers relates to his own experience of alienation from his father. Much of Stephen's Hamlet theory seems to develop out of his own life, and we see Stephen thinking about parallel personal matters—his mother, his sexuality, and so on— while he argues about Shakespeare's life and work.

The cameo appearances of Bloom in this episode remind us of the sonless Bloom's suitability as a replacement father figure for Stephen. The schematics of the chapter reinforce this sense. Though Stephen himself seems to be the Odysseus figure for a time in the "Scylla and Charybdis" episode, in the schematic of Shakespeare, Bloom seems to be the father figure (Shakespeare) and Stephen, the son (Hamlet). Bloom is aligned with Shakespeare through their similarly unfaithful wives and dead sons, Hamnet and Rudy, respectively. As Shakespeare writes the drama of his wife into his art, so did we see Bloom consider writing a story based on Molly at the end of Episode Four.

# EPISODE TEN:
# "THE WANDERING ROCKS"

## SUMMARY
Episode Ten consists of nineteen short views of characters, major and minor, as they make their way around Dublin in the afternoon. Within each subsection, short, disjunctive paragraphs pop up that depict a simultaneous action in some other part of the city. These are not rendered below.

Father John Conmee travels from his Dublin presbytery to a suburban school to try to get Patrick Dignam's son admitted for free. Conmee walks to the tram station, passing a one-legged sailor, three schoolboys, and others on the way. Conmee gets on an outbound tram, notices a poster of Eugene Stratton, a blackface minstrel, and thinks about missionary work. Conmee gets off at Howth road, takes out his breviary (book of prayers), and reads to himself as he walks. In front of him, a young couple guiltily emerges from the hedgerow. Conmee blesses them.

Corny Kelleher examines a coffinlid, then gossips with a policeman.

The one-legged sailor crutches up Eccles street, singing a patriotic English song and asking for alms. He passes Katey and Boody Dedalus. A woman's arm (Molly's) throws a coin out of a window for the sailor.

Katey and Boody Dedalus enter their kitchen, where their sister Maggy is washing clothes. The Dedalus sisters discuss the household's lack of money and food—Sister Mary Patrick has donated some pea soup to them. Maggy explains that Dilly has gone to see their father, Simon Dedalus.

The throwaway that Bloom threw into the river in Episode Eight floats down river.

A shopgirl arranges a basket of food for Blazes Boylan. Boylan writes the delivery address and looks down the girl's shirt. He takes a red flower for his lapel and asks to use her telephone.

Stephen meets his voice teacher, Almidano Artifoni, in the street outside Trinity College. Artifoni tries to persuade Stephen to pursue a music career in Dublin. Stephen is flattered. Artifoni runs to catch a tram.

Miss Dunne, Blazes Boylan's secretary, puts away the novel she is reading. She daydreams about going out tonight. Boylan calls. Miss Dunne tells Boylan that Lenehan will be at the Ormond Hotel at four o'clock.

Ned Lambert meets with J.J. O'Molloy and the reverend Hugh C. Love to show the reverend around Saint Mary's Abbey (now Lambert's warehouse). Lambert discusses the history of the abbey with Love, who is writing a history book. Lambert and O'Molloy discuss O'Molloy's money troubles.

Tom Rochford shows his invention, a mechanism to keep track of betting races, to Nosey Flynn, McCoy, and Lenehan. Lenehan promises to speak to Boylan this afternoon about Rochford's invention. McCoy and Lenehan leave together. Lenehan ducks into a betting office to check on the price for Sceptre, his pick for the Gold Cup race. Lenehan re-emerges and reports to McCoy that Bantam Lyons is inside betting on a long-shot horse (the horse Lyons thinks Bloom tipped him to in Episode Five). The men spot Bloom looking through a book merchant's cart nearby. Lenehan claims to have groped a willing Molly. McCoy sticks up for Bloom, who he thinks has an artistic side.

Bloom looks through the books at a bookseller's cart and settles on *Sweets of Sin* for Molly.

At Dillon's auction rooms, the lacquey rings the bell. Dilly Dedalus waits outside for her father. Simon emerges and Dilly asks him for money. He hands over a shilling he borrowed from Jack Power. Dilly suspects he has more money, but Simon walks away from her.

The viceregal cavalcade has begun its cross-town journey.

Tom Kernan passes the spot where the patriot Robert Emmet was hanged, and thinks of Ben Dollard singing "The Croppy Boy." Kernan spots the viceregal cavalcade, but waves too late.

Stephen looks at jewels in a shop window, then browses a book-seller's cart. His sister Dilly approaches him and asks Stephen if a French primer that she just bought is good. Stephen considers Dilly, who has his eyes and his quick mind but who is caught in the desperate situation at their family home. Stephen is caught between an impulse to save Dilly and the others and an impulse to escape from them completely.

Bob Cowley greets Simon Dedalus and they discuss Cowley's debt to Reuben J. Dodd, the moneylender. Ben Dollard arrives with advice about Cowley's debt.

Martin Cunningham, along with Jack Power and John Wyse Nolan, conducts a collection for the Dignam children. Nolan ironically notes Bloom's generous five-shilling donation. Cunningham, Power, and Nolan meet up with John Henry, the assistant town clerk, and John Fanning, the subsheriff. The viceregal cavalcade passes them.

Buck Mulligan and Haines sit in a coffeeshop, where Parnell's brother is playing chess in the corner. Haines and Mulligan discuss Stephen—Haines thinks Stephen is mentally off-balance. Mulligan agrees that Stephen will never turn out to be a true poet, because he has been damaged by Catholic visions of hell.

Tisdall Farrell walks behind Almidano Artifoni in a zigzag and collides with the blind man that Bloom helped at the end of Episode Eight.

Dignam's son, Patrick junior, walks homeward carrying porksteaks. He passes other schoolboys and wonders if they know of his father's death. He thinks of his father's coffin being carried out and the last time he saw his father, who was drunk and going out to the pub.

The progress of the viceregal cavalcade (containing William Humble, Earl of Dudley and Lady Dudley, among others) is tracked, from the viceregal lodge in Phoenix park to the Mirus bazaar. It passes many of the people we have seen so far in the chapter. Most of them notice, and some salute the cavalcade.

---

ANALYSIS

Episode Ten, "The Wandering Rocks," serves as an interlude between the first and last nine episodes. The technique of the episode is somewhat filmic. The episode as a whole renders the sense of a wide view of the entire city of Dublin, with figures moving throughout, while the nineteen subsections, and the cut-aways within them, function as quickly changing close-ups. Accordingly, much of the episode is focused on exteriors—appearances and movements. Few characters are granted more than a line or two of interior monologue. The "Wandering Rocks" of *The Odyssey* were apparently boulders that shifted position in the mist and could capsize a ship (Odysseus never actually sailed through them). Joyce's "Wandering Rocks" in Episode Ten are represented by textual traps for the reader. The most common type of trap is the one- or two-line interpolations that suddenly describe action happening elsewhere. These textual traps make the narrator seem particularly masterful or obtuse.

The episode is framed on each end by an extended progression—Father Conmee's trip to a suburban school at the beginning, and the viceregal cavalcade's progress from Phoenix Park to the Mirus bazaar at the end. Both are on altruistic errands—Conmee is trying to get Dignam's son into Jesuit school for free, and the Earl of Dudley is presiding over the Mirus charity bazaar to benefit Mercer's Hospital. Individually, they represent the power of religious and governmental institutions.

We get a closer view of Stephen's family in this episode. Stephen is not currently sleeping at home, where his sisters, Maggy, Katey, Boody, and Dilly, struggle to provide subsistence for themselves and the rest of the family since their mother has died. Stephen's run-in with Dilly at the bookseller's stall shows Stephen experiencing remorse about his family, especially because Dilly shows a spark of intellect similar to his own. Yet he has just received a paycheck today, and it has been and will be spent on drink, like his father's money. Stephen refuses to succumb to his conscience and be dragged back into the despair of his family's poverty and misery.

Bloom and Stephen, though they do not meet, are further aligned in this episode. We see both men browsing a bookseller's cart (both, interestingly, look at books about sex). Both men do not see the viceregal cavalcade at the end, though most of the other characters do. We see other characters gossiping about Stephen and Bloom, specifically referencing their artistic sensibilities. McCoy tells Lenehan that Bloom has a refined, artistic side, while Buck tells Haines that, though he will never be a poet, Stephen will write something in ten years. This schematic alignment of Stephen and Bloom prepares us for their climactic meeting to come and prepares us to see their "relationship" as potentially something other than father-son.

## EPISODE ELEVEN: "SIRENS"

### SUMMARY

Episode Eleven begins with a jumbled prelude of phrases—fragments, it turns out, of the text to come. Episode Eleven also uses a technique simlar to Episode Ten, whereby sections of text that describe events happening in another location interrupt the narrative at hand.

The Ormond Hotel barmaids, Lydia Douce and Mina Kennedy, strain to see the viceregal cavalcade out the window, then gossip and giggle over their tea. Meanwhile, Bloom is walking past shop windows nearby.

Simon Dedalus enters the Ormond bar, followed by Lenehan, looking for Boylan. The barmaids serve them drinks and discuss the blind piano tuner who tuned the Ormond piano earlier today. Dedalus tests out the piano in the saloon. Boylan arrives and flirts with Miss Kennedy while he and Lenehan await the wire results of the Gold Cup race.

In the meantime, while buying notepaper to write to Martha, Bloom has noticed Boylan's jaunty car on Essex Bridge. Mindful of Boylan's fast-approaching four o'clock rendezvous with Molly, Bloom decides to follow the car to the Ormond Hotel. Outside the hotel, Bloom runs into Richie Goulding and agrees to have dinner with him inside— Bloom plans to survey Boylan. They sit down in the dining room.

Boylan and Lenehan, leaving, pass Bob Cowley and Ben Dollard on their way in. In the dining room, Pat the waiter takes Goulding's and Bloom's drink orders. Bloom hears the jingle of Boylan's car pulling away and nearly sobs with anxiety. In the saloon, Dedalus and Dollard reminisce about past vocal concerts and the time Dollard had to borrow evening clothes from the Blooms' second-hand clothing shop for a performance. The men discuss Molly appreciatively. In the dining room, Bloom, too, is thinking about Molly, as Pat serves dinner.

Interspersed with these passages are the jingle of Boylan's car and updates on its progress toward the Blooms'.

Ben Dollard sings "Love and War," and Bloom recognizes it from the dining room. He thinks of the night that Dollard borrowed evening wear from Molly's shop. In the saloon, Dedalus is encouraged to sing "*M'appari,*" the tenor's song from *Martha.*

Goulding reminisces about opera performances. Bloom thinks sympathetically about Goulding's chronic back pain and unsympathetically about Goulding's tendency to lie. In the saloon, Dedalus begins to sing "*M'appari.*" Goulding recognizes Dedalus singing. Bloom thinks of Dedalus's vocal talent, wasted by drinking. Bloom realizes the song is from *Martha*—a coincidence, as he was just about to write to Martha Clifford. Touched by the music, Bloom reminisces about his first fateful meeting with Molly. The song ends to applause. Tom Kernan enters the bar.

Bloom muses on the Dedalus-Goulding falling-out. Ruminating on the melancholy lyrics of "*M'appari,*" Bloom thinks about death and Dignam's funeral this morning. Bloom thinks to himself about the mathematics of music, and how Milly has no taste in music.

Bloom begins writing a letter to Martha. He covers the page with his newspaper and tells Goulding he is answering an advertisement. Bloom writes flirtatious lines and encloses a half-crown. Bloom feels bored with the correspondence.

A recurring "tap" begins here—it is the tap of the blind piano tuner's walking stick. He is returning to retrieve his tuning fork.

Bloom watches Miss Douce flirt at the bar. Cowley plays the minuet of *Don Giovanni.* Bloom thinks about the omnipresence of music in the world, women's singing voices, and the eroticism of acoustic music. He imagines that Boylan is just arriving to meet Molly. Indeed, Boylan is now knocking on the Blooms' door.

Tom Kernan requests "The Croppy Boy" (a nationalist song about a young member of the 1798 rebellion tricked and hanged by a British man disguised as his confession priest). Bloom prepares to leave—Goulding is disappointed. All are quiet for the song. Bloom watches Miss Douce and wonders if she notices him looking at her. Bloom hears the line about the Croppy Boy being the last of his race and thinks about his own stunted family line.

Bloom continues watching Miss Douce, who is running her hand around the phallic beer-pull. Bloom finally rouses himself. He bids Goulding goodbye, checks his belongings, and dodges out to the hallway before cheers erupt at the end of the song.

Bloom walks toward the post office, feeling gassy from the cider. He regrets making a five o'clock appointment to meet Cunningham about the Dignams' insurance. Bloom thinks skeptically that the Croppy Boy should have noticed that the priest was a British soldier in disguise.

Back at the Ormond, someone mentions to Dedalus that Bloom was there and just left—they discuss Bloom and Molly's vocal talent. The blind piano tuner finally arrives to retrieve his tuning fork.

Bloom spots Bridie Kelly, a local prostitute with whom he once had an encounter. He avoids her by looking in a shop window at a picture of Irish patriot Robert Emmet and his famous last words. Bloom reads the speech to himself, while farting under the cover of a noisily approaching tram.

---

## ANALYSIS

In the *Odyssey*, Odysseus orders his men to tie him to the mast of his ship and to plug their own ears so that they will not succumb to the beautiful song of the sirens and be diverted to their deaths. Odysseus chooses to be bound and to keep his ears unplugged because he cannot bear the idea of *not* hearing the sirens' music. Episode Eleven of *Ulysses* accordingly focuses on music. The episode takes place around four o'clock and onward in the afternoon, at the Ormond bar-restaurant where Simon Dedalus, Ben Dollard, and Bob Cowley entertain the small afternoon dinner crowd with opera love songs and a nationalist ballad. The narrative style reinforces the focus on music. The opening section of disjunctive phrases work as a sort of musical overture or warm-up. The interspersed "jingle" of Boylan's car, combined with the recurring "tap" sound of the blind piano tuner's cane, provide a sort of underlying rhythm section to the episode proper.

The sirens themselves are in part represented by the beautiful, flirtatious barmaids. Bloom is enticed by their charms, especially toward the end of the episode, when he stays longer than intended, watching Miss Douce. The sirens are also represented, though, by Simon Dedalus, Ben Dollard, and Bob Cowley in the saloon. Their renditions of longing love songs hold the entire bar and dining area in thrall. Bloom's mind is captivated by the emotional songs, and whenever there is a break in their performance, Bloom longs again for the music to distract him from thoughts of Molly and Boylan. Yet Dedalus, Dollard, and Cowley are each past their prime and represent the descent into death. Unmarried or widowed, they represent Bloom's worst fears about himself as the last of his family line. Just as Ulysses and his men escape, so does Bloom ultimately resist the pull of the music at the end of the episode by rejecting its increasingly sentimental verses and leaving before the self-congratulatory ending of "The Croppy Boy."

The technique of the third-person narrative changes with Episode Eleven to become self-conscious and playful. As we began to see in Episode Ten, the narrative seems to be arranging bits of "objective" reporting to create specific meaning, as when Bloom walking is juxtaposed with the old "fogey" that the barmaids laugh over in the opening scene of the episode, to maliciously suggest Bloom's unattractiveness. The narrative now calls attention to itself as one big text, with its purposeful repetition of earlier narrative phrases. The narrative makes the borders of

SUMMARY & ANALYSIS

disparate episodes, characters, and monologue-narrative bleed together.

Parts of Stephen's interior monologue inexplicably re-emerge here in Episode Eleven; names become a source of humor as the two men who order tankards of beer are labeled "tankards," and the overflowing feelings introduced by Dedalus's song are rendered by a series of composite names such as "Siopold." The narrative itself is becoming increasingly part of the plot, rather than the transparent medium that communicates the plot. This prepares us for upcoming episodes in which the tone of the narrative will dictate what exactly can be said and what cannot—forcing us to analyze this interference and evaluate how the narrative style effects our understanding of the plot.

The "Sirens" episode is generally seen to represent a turning point in Bloom's attitude toward Boylan and Molly's impending affair. Bloom coincidentally sees Boylan for the third time today. Instead of hiding, as he has done on the previous two occasions, Bloom resolves to follow Boylan and even to enter the Ormond hotel and watch his movements. Though the two men do not actually have a confrontation in Episode Eleven, the emphasis on the off-stage drama of Molly and Boylan's rendezvous, combined with the love-and-war themed songs, lends a climactic feel to the episode.

## EPISODE TWELVE: "CYCLOPS"

> —*A nation? says Bloom. A nation is the same people living in the same place.*     (See QUOTATIONS, p. 83)

### SUMMARY

An unnamed, first-person narrator describes the events of his afternoon. In addition to the first-person narration, the episode contains over thirty passages in prose that parody—through hyperbole—Irish mythology, legal jargon, journalism, and the Bible, among other things.

The narrator meets Joe Hynes on the street, and agrees to get a drink at Barney Kiernan's pub so Hynes can tell the citizen about the foot-and-mouth disease cattle meeting. A passage in the style of old Celtic sagas describes the marketplace they walk past as a land of plenty. Arriving at the pub, they greet the citizen and his dog, Garryowen. The citizen is described at length, mock-heroically.

Alf Bergan enters, laughing at Denis Breen, who is walking by outside with his wife. Bergan tells the story of Breen's "U.p: up" postcard and orders a Guinness from the bartender. The beverage is lovingly described. The citizen notices Bloom pacing outside and wonders with hostility what he is doing—he refers to Bloom as a freemason.

Talk switches to Paddy Dignam. A seance at which Dignam's soul appears is described. Bob Doran (a character from *Dubliners*) rails loudly at the cruelty of God to take Dignam away. The narrator disgust-edly notes that Doran is on his annual drinking binge.

Bloom enters—he is supposed to meet Martin Cunningham. Hynes tries to buy Bloom a drink, but Bloom politely refuses. The subject of hangings is raised, and Bloom speaks pedantically about capital punish-ment. The citizen dominates the conversation, recalling hanged Irish nationalists. The narrator watches Bloom and thinks scornfully of Molly—the narrator knows a fair amount about the Blooms, thanks to Pisser Burke, who has a connection to them. Bloom is trying to make a fine point about hangings, but the citizen interrupts him with narrow-minded nationalistic sentiments. A passage of journalistic prose describes the public spectacle of a martyr's hanging.

Hynes orders another round. The narrator is bitter that Bloom will not drink nor buy rounds. Bloom explains he is meeting Cunningham to visit Mrs. Dignam. Bloom launches into an explanation of the insurance complexities.

The men briefly discuss Nannetti, who is running for mayor, and the citizen denounces Nanetti's Italian origins. The conversation switches to sports: Hynes alludes to the citizen's role as a founder of the Gaelic sports revival. Bergan mentions a recent boxing match from which Boy-lan profited. Bloom talks about lawn tennis while everyone else dis-cusses Boylan. A sports journalese passage describes an Irish-English boxing match. Bergan brings up Boylan's and Molly's upcoming con-cert tour. Bloom is distant, and the narrator guesses that Boylan is sleep-ing with Molly.

J.J. O'Molloy and Ned Lambert enter. Conversation switches to Denis Breen's madness—Bloom ponders Mrs. Breen's suffering, but no one else is sympathetic. The citizen, involved in a conversation about Ireland's troubles, begins making anti-Semitic and xenophobic remarks while looking at Bloom. Bloom ignores him.

John Wyse Nolan and Lenehan enter. Lenehan tells the narrator about the Gold Cup race. Throwaway, an outside horse won—Lene-han, Boylan, and Boylan's "lady friend" lost money on Sceptre. The citizen continues declaring the exploitation of Ireland—he longs for the day when Ireland can respond to the wrongs England has committed against it with force.

Bloom contends that persecution perpetuates nationalistic hatred. Nolan and the citizen quiz Bloom about his own nationality. Bloom claims Irish nationality by birth and Jewish allegiance. Nolan suggests that the Jews have not properly stood up for themselves. Bloom responds that love and life are better options than force and hatred. Bloom leaves to go find Cunningham. The citizen ridicules Bloom's call for love.

Lenehan tells everyone Bloom probably went to cash in on his Throwaway bet (see Episode Five for this misunderstanding). The narrator visits the outhouse, thinking disparagingly about Bloom's stingi-ness. He returns inside to find everyone gossiping about Bloom.

Cunningham, Power, and Crofton arrive. A Renaissance-style pas-sage describes the greetings. Cunningham asks for Bloom, and the new arrivals quickly become involved in the Bloom-gossiping. Cunningham reveals Bloom's Hungarian origins and original family name, Virag. The citizen sarcastically suggests that Bloom is the new Messiah for Ire-land. He jokingly suggests that Bloom's children are not his own, then alludes to Bloom's femininity. Cunningham calls for charity toward Bloom and toasts a blessing to all present. A passage describing the blessing ceremony follows.

Bloom re-enters the pub breathlessly to find that Cunningham has arrived. Cunningham, sensing that the room is turning belligerent, escorts Bloom, Power, and Crofton out to their car. The citizen follows, yelling jibes about Bloom's Jewishness. The narrator is disgusted with the citizen for making a scene. Bloom, held back by Power, lists off famous Jews, including, finally, Christ. The citizen grabs a biscuit tin and throws it after the car. A long passage provides an exaggerated description of the impact of the tin. A biblical passage describes Bloom as Elijah in a chariot ascending into heaven.

## ANALYSIS

Episode Twelve corresponds to the adventure in which Odysseus and his men become trapped in the cave of Cyclops, a one-eyed monster. Cyclops seems to be represented by both the narrator and the citizen. The narrator's biased first-person ("I") viewpoint renders him Cyclops-like. But it is the citizen who is the most clear representation of the bel-ligerent, one-eyed monster. The citizen's one-eyed quality is his partic-ularly uncompromising, narrow-minded, and xenophobic brand of Irish nationalism. In contrast to the citizen's one-eyed presence, Bloom remains distinctly two-eyed—able to consider more than one side of an issue and to reconcile two viewpoints by compromise.

Bloom's ability to be moderate in the face of the citizen's excessive-ness is part of what makes him a target for the men in this episode. Bloom stands out in several ways. He does not drink, and thus refuses the friendly economy of standing drinks and having drinks bought for him. He repeatedly turns the easy-going bar conversation serious with his intellectual superiority. Yet Bloom seems to have been targeted before even entering the bar. As the episode continues, Bloom alone stands up to the citizen's excessive viewpoints, and Bloom's eccentrici-ties (and rumors about his personal affairs) become synonymous with his Jewishness to the other men, as the atmosphere becomes increas-ingly anti-Semitic.

Episode Twelve, "Cyclops," represents the climax of all the public chapters of *Ulysses*—all the tensions that have been building around Bloom in the other social episodes come to a head. Here, also, for the first time, we do not get any interior monologue from either Stephen or Bloom. Instead of our usual third-person narrator, a first-person, unnamed narrator gives a biased view of events at Barney Kiernan's with his own satiric commentary. In addition to the narrator's first-person commentaries, thirty-two interspersed passages of inflated prose recall a variety of styles. These interpolations are unique so far in *Ulysses* because they seem to change the setting of the episode—they depart from Barney Kiernan's to describe scenes as diverse as a court trial, a parliamentary session, and a public hanging. They give us a sense of what is to come in the novel, specifically the dream-like sequence of Episode Fifteen. Though the styles and settings of the thirty-two passages differ, they are similar in their hyperbolic quality. None of the scenes are realistic—all are exaggerated to hilarious degree, some containing lists that span more than half a page. They render their subjects laughable, and in their affiliation with the citizen's own inflated, excessive, unstoppable rhetoric, they render him laughable as well.

The citizen here represents a particular kind of Irish nationalism that bases itself on an idea of racial purity. The citizen's "us-versus-them" logic allows him to sustain his single-minded, one-eyed personal and national mission. The citizen is able to recognize the brutality and moral bankruptcy underlying the British Empire, yet he cannot recognize these same qualities in Irish society. Here, the hyperbolic passages step in to reinforce the satire, as when prose resembling that of a newspaper's society page describes a Dublin crowd's glee and sentimentality at a public hanging. Similarly, the citizen's blindness will not allow him to see that just as Bloom does not buy drinks for the crowd, neither does the citizen himself. But Bloom's refusal to stand drinks is codified as a Jewish trait and used to mark him as different and inferior. Against this one-eyed perspective stands the fluid symbolism of *Ulysses* itself, in which Bloom figures as an Irishman, a Jew, and a Greek (Odysseus).

The symbolism of Episode Twelve increasingly uses Christian imagery to depict Bloom as a Christ-figure or an Elijah-figure, as others seek to crucify Bloom or sacrifice him as a scapegoat. These analogies further suggest an underdog figure victorious in the end. This representation connects with the symbolism of the Gold Cup horserace in which Throwaway, the underdog horse that Bloom supposedly tipped Bantam Lyons to, comes from behind to win the race against Sceptre, the horse on which Lenehan and Boylan have bet. Because Bloom is distanced from Sceptre, the phallic and violent connotations of the horse's name reinforce his position as a non-violent, effeminate, self-sacrificing outsider.

# EPISODE THIRTEEN: "NAUSICAA"

## SUMMARY

A mawkish, clichéd, third-person narrative describes the summer evening on Sandymount Strand, near Mary, Star of the Sea church. Bloom stands across the beach from three girlfriends—Cissy Caffrey, Edy Boardman, and Gerty MacDowell—and their charges: Cissy's twin toddler brothers and Edy's baby brother. Cissy and Edy tend to the babies and occasionally tease Gerty, who is sitting some distance away. The narrative sympathetically describes Gerty as beautiful, and outlines the commercial products she uses to maintain her looks. Gerty's crush—the boy who bicycles past her house—has been aloof lately. Gerty daydreams of marriage and domestic life with a silent, strong man. Meanwhile, Edy and Cissy deal loudly with the children's disputes. Gerty is mortified by her friends' unladylike obscenity, especially in front of the gentleman (Bloom). Nearby, at the Star of the Sea church, a men's temperance retreat begins with a supplication to the Virgin.

The toddlers kick their ball too far. Bloom picks it up and throws it back—the ball rolls to a stop under Gerty's skirt. Gerty tries to kick the ball to Cissy but misses. Gerty senses Bloom's eyes on her and notices his sad face. She fantasizes that he is a foreigner in mourning who needs her comfort. Gerty displays her ankles and her hair for Bloom, knowing she is arousing him.

Gerty wonders aloud how late it is, hoping Cissy and Edy will take the children home. Cissy approaches Bloom and asks for the time. Bloom's watch has stopped. Gerty watches Bloom put his hands back in his pockets and senses the onset of her menstrual cycle. She yearns to know Bloom's story—is he married? A widower? Duty-bound to a madwoman?

Cissy and the others are preparing to leave when the fireworks from the Mirus bazaar begin. They run down the strand to watch, but Gerty remains. Gerty leans back, holding her knee in her hands, knowingly revealing her legs, while she watches a "long Roman candle" firework shoot high in the sky. At the climax of the episode and Gerty's emotions (and Bloom's own orgasmic climax, we soon realize) the Roman candle bursts in the air, to cries of "O! O!" on the ground.

As Gerty rises and begins to walk to the others, Bloom realizes that she is lame in one foot. He feels shock and pity, then relief that he did not know this when she was arousing him. Bloom ponders the sexual appeal of abnormalities, then women's sexual urges as heightened by their menstrual cycles. Remembering Gerty's two friends, he considers the competitiveness of female friendships, like Molly's with Josie Breen. Bloom remembers that his watch was stopped at 4:30, and he wonders if that is when Molly and Boylan had sex.

Bloom rearranges his semen-stained shirt and ponders strategies for seducing women. Bloom wonders if Gerty noticed him masturbating—he guesses that she did, as women are very aware. He briefly wonders if Gerty is Martha Clifford. Bloom thinks about how soon girls become mothers, then of Mrs. Purefoy at the nearby maternity hospital. Bloom ponders the "magnetism" that could account for his watch stopping when Boylan and Molly were together, perhaps the same magnetism that draws men and women together.

Bloom smells Gerty's perfume in the air—a cheap smell, not like Molly's complex scent, opoponax. Bloom smells inside his waistcoat, wondering what a man's smell would be. The scent of the lemon soap reminds him that he forgot to pick up Molly's lotion.

A "nobleman" passes Bloom. Bloom wonders about the man and considers writing a story called "The Mystery Man on the Beach." This thought reminds him of the macintosh man at Dignam's funeral. Looking at Howth lighthouse, Bloom considers the science of light and colors, then the day he and Molly spent there. Now, Boylan is with her. Bloom feels drained. He notices that Mass seems to be over. The postman makes his nine o'clock round with a lamp. A newsboy cries the results of the Gold Cup race.

Bloom decides to avoid going home just yet. He reconsiders the incident in Barney Kiernan's— perhaps the citizen meant no harm. Bloom thinks about his evening visit to Mrs. Dignam. Bloom tries to remember his dream last night. Molly was dressed in Turkish breeches and red slippers.

Bloom picks up a stray piece of paper, then a stick. Wondering if Gerty will return tomorrow, he begins to write her a message in the sand—"I AM A"—but stops as there is not sufficient room. He erases the letters and throws the stick, which lands straight up in the sand. He decides to have a short nap, and his thoughts become muddled by sleep. Bloom dozes off as a cuckoo clock chimes in the priest's house nearby.

---

## ANALYSIS

In Episode Thirteen of *Ulysses*, Gerty MacDowell corresponds to Princess Nausicaa, who, in *The Odyssey,* discovers Odysseus asleep on the beach and tends to him. Gerty, associated with blue and white, also seems to correspond to the Virgin Mary. Sounds from the nearby temperance retreat are interspersed with Gerty's narrative, creating an ironic parallel between Gerty and Mary: as Gerty dreams of ministering to a husband and opens herself to Bloom's supplicating sexual attention, so do the men in the church appeal to the statue of the Virgin Mary for comfort and aid. Episode Thirteen is the first episode of *Ulysses* that centers on a female consciousness, and it inaugurates the final sections of the book, which are more female-centered in their characters and settings.

The first half of Episode Thirteen centers on Gerty's appearance and consciousness, and we only hear Bloom's interior monologue in the second half of the episode. Gerty's half consists of several barely distinct narrative points of view and styles. The narrative is sympathetic with Gerty, and Gerty's consciousness slides in and out of the narrative—her interior monologue is sometimes rendered directly. The narrative's style borrows from (and parodies) the prose of both moralizing, sentimental literature and consumer-oriented women's magazines. The style is accordingly full of emotional clichés, effusive diction, and imprecise descriptions. Additionally, the style of the narrative is such that unpleasant realities and indelicate details are filtered out. Thus, Gerty's lame foot is only slightly alluded to, as is masturbation.

The feminine pleasantries and the focus on sentimental love in Episode Thirteen seem to be something of a response to Episode Twelve's masculine violence and prejudice. This hypothesis fits with the workings of *Ulysses,* by which previous perspectives are tempered by later styles and character viewpoints. Thus, Bloom's foreignness—a detriment in Episode Twelve—becomes an attractive asset for him in Episode Thirteen. Yet Episodes Twelve and Thirteen ultimately turn out to have straightforward affinities. Excess lacking substance seems common to both, from the hyperbolic lists of Episode Twelve to the lush expositions of Episode Thirteen. And both episodes seem to offer examples of categorical or stereotypical thinking. The citizen's logic worked on the seemingly straightforward basis of race and religion. Gerty's thoughts offer conventional ideas, while the narrative of Episode Thirteen invites us to evaluate Gerty as an entirely typical Irish girl.

Women in Episode Thirteen are defined, in part, by their perceptiveness about who is looking at them and when. Women become sexual beings through their ability to present themselves to be looked at, and Bloom's erotic moments are voyeuristic. Stephen, in "Proteus," experimented with closing his eyes and concentrating on his other senses. The second half of Episode Thirteen reflects a shift of emphasis from the eyes to the nose. Bloom's thoughts hover around smells and smelling. The distinction between the emphasis on senses in the two beach episodes seems to lie in the import of Stephen's and Bloom's musings— Stephen seeks to understand how our senses order our relationship to the physical world, while Bloom's thoughts dwell on sight and smelling as ordering relationships between people.

Like the other women whom Bloom has seen and fantasized about so far in *Ulysses,* Gerty eventually reminds Bloom of Molly, suggesting that Bloom's desire for Molly is often refracted through another woman. It is in this episode that Bloom notices for the first time that his watch has stopped, apparently sometime between four and five o'clock—perhaps at the exact time of Boylan and Molly's tryst. Yet our sympathy for Bloom's sadness at this thought is tempered by the circumstances of the discovery—Bloom himself is conducting a tryst at this later hour, albeit an unconsummated one.

# EPISODE FOURTEEN: "OXEN OF THE SUN"

## SUMMARY

The narrative technique of Episode Fourteen is meant to represent the gestation of the English language. The prose styles of many different time periods, along with the styles of their most famous authors, are replicated and at times parodied in chronological order.

Latinate prose, and then alliterative Anglo-Saxon, situate us at the Holles Street maternity hospital, run by Sir Andrew Horne. Bloom arrives at the hospital gates, having come to check on Mrs. Purefoy. Nurse Callan, an acquaintance of Bloom's, opens the gate and leads him inside. Their conversation about Mrs. Purefoy, who has been in labor for three days, is described in moralizing medieval prose. The emergence of Dixon, a medical student, from a noisy room down the hall is described in medieval-romance style. Dixon, who once treated Bloom for a bee sting, invites Bloom inside, where Lenehan, Crotthers, Stephen, Punch Costello, and medical students Lynch and Madden are boisterously gathered around a spread of sardines and beer. Dixon pours Bloom a beer, which Bloom quietly deposits in his neighbor's cup. A nun comes to the door and asks for quiet.

The men discuss medical cases in which the doctor must choose between saving the mother or the baby—Stephen discusses the religious aspect of this question while others joke about contraception and sex. Bloom is somber, thinking of Mrs. Purefoy and of Molly's labor with Rudy. Bloom considers Stephen, imagining that he is wasting time with these men.

Stephen's pouring of more beer and consideration of the quibbles of Mary's pregnancy with Jesus are described in Elizabethan prose. Punch Costello interrupts with a bawdy song about a pregnant woman. Nurse Quigley comes to the door and shushes them. The men's teasing Stephen about the piety of his youth is described in early seventeenth-century prose. A thunderclap erupts. Bloom notices that Stephen is truly frightened at this evidence of God's anger, and he attempts to calm Stephen by explaining the science of thunder.

Buck Mulligan's meeting with Alec Bannon on the street nearby is described in seventeenth-century diary style. Alec tells Buck about a girl he is dating in Mullingar (Milly Bloom). The two men walk together to the hospital on Holles street.

The good-for-nothing characters of Lenehan and Costello are described in the prose style of Daniel Defoe. The subject of Deasy's letter and cattle health is broached. A long, allegorical joke ensues about papal bulls, Henry VIII, and England's relationship to Ireland. Buck's arrival is described in Addison's and Steele's essay style. Buck jokes about his new occupation as a "fertiliser" for all female comers. A side conversation between Crotthers and Bannon about Milly, and Bannon's intent to purchase contraception in Dublin, is described in Lawrence Sterne's style. The men euphemistically discuss different contraceptive methods.

The eighteenth-century style of Oliver Goldsmith follows. Nurse Callan summons Dixon: Mrs. Purefoy has borne a son. The men licentiously discuss Nurse Callan. Eighteenth-century political prose style is used to describe Bloom's relief at the news of Mrs. Purefoy's baby, and his disgust with the young men's manner. The satirical style of Junius queries Bloom's hypocritically self-righteous attitude toward the medical students.

Edward Gibbon's style is used to describe the men's conversation about various topics related to birth: Caesarean sections, fathers who die before their wives give birth, cases of fratricide (including the Childs murder case, mentioned in Episode Six), artificial insemination, menopause, impregnation by rape, birthmarks, Siamese twins. Gothic prose is employed to describe Buck telling a ghost story.

Charles Lamb's sentimental style is utilized to describe Bloom reminiscing about himself as a young man, then feeling paternal toward the young men. The hazy, hallucinatory style of Thomas DeQuincey manifests the pessimistic turn Bloom's thoughts suddenly take. Walter Savage Landor's prose style is incorporated to describe how Lenehan and Lynch manage to offend Stephen by broaching the topics of his fruitless poetic career and his dead mother. Conversation switches to the Gold Cup race, then to Lynch's girlfriend Kitty; we learn that Lynch and Kitty were the couple caught by Father Conmee this afternoon (in Episode Ten).

Nineteenth-century historical and naturalist styles follow. The conversation turns to the mysterious causes of infant mortality. Charles Dickens's sentimental style is used to describe Mrs. Purefoy, joyous mother.

Cardinal Newman's religious prose style is employed to describe how past sins can haunt a man. Walter Pater's aestheticist style follows. Bloom ponders Stephen's aggressive words about mothers and babies. Bloom remembers watching Stephen, as a child, exchange reproachful glances with his mother. John Ruskin's style is used to describe Stephen's spontaneous suggestion to proceed to Burke's pub. Dixon joins them. Bloom lags behind, asking Nurse Callan to say a kind word to Mrs. Purefoy. Thomas Carlyle's prose style hails the virility of Mr. Purefoy.

The narrative breaks into a chaotic rendering of various twentieth-century dialect and slang as the men hurry to Burke's. Stephen buys the first round. The Gold Cup race is discussed, Stephen buys another round of absinthe, and Alec Bannon finally realizes that Bloom is Milly's father and nervously slips away. The barman calls time, and someone gossips about the man in the macintosh in the corner. The barman kicks them out as the Fire Brigade passes on its way to a fire. Someone vomits. Stephen convinces Lynch to come with him to the brothel district. A nearby poster advertising a visiting minister (the same ad that Bloom received in Episode Eight) inspires a final switch to the style of American sales-pitch evangelism.

---

## ANALYSIS

The style of Episode Fourteen, one of the most difficult in the novel, consists of imitations of chronological stages in the growth of the English language, beginning with Latinate and Middle English prose up to the chaos of twentieth-century slang. The progression of language is, in turn, meant to correspond to the nine-month gestation period leading to human birth. The imitations of the styles of different time periods and prominent writers seem parodic because the styles are somewhat exaggerated (some more so than others). The ultimate effect is to drive home the point that has been made more subtly in Episodes Twelve and Thirteen: narrative style contains built-in ideology that effects what is reported and how it is reported. Joyce shows this by allowing each different style to gravitate toward its normal subject matter. Thus, the moral-allegorical style of John Bunyan explores Stephen's move away from the piety of his youth; Defoe's passage is spent describing the no-gooders Lenehan and Costello; and the sentimental style of Charles Dickens narrates the commendably maternal thoughts of Mina Purefoy. The differing moral judgments expressed by various styles are also highlighted—Bloom's compassion is venerated in the Middle English prose section, while the hypocrisy of Bloom's disapproval (of the young men) is harshly revealed in the satirical prose style of Junius.

Episode Fourteen, "Oxen of the Sun," corresponds to Odysseus's visit to the island of Helios in the *Odyssey*. Odysseus warns his men not to touch the cattle that are sacred to Helios, but the men slaughter the cattle for food while Odysseus is asleep. Zeus avenges Helios—only Odysseus lives, and his voyage home to Ithaca is further delayed. Joyce highlights the correspondence in part through a host of cattle imagery and mainly through the theme of profaning the sacred. Joyce's Episode Fourteen, which takes place in a maternity hospital during the birth of Mina Purefoy's son, concentrates on fertility. The theme of the profaning of the sacred is thus represented by the blasphemous discussion of pregnancy and birth.

In the larger setting of the maternity hospital, as well as the smaller setting of the revelrous gathering of medical students and friends, the personal, private, and female aspects of pregnancy and birth are obscured, while the social, clinical, political, legal, and economic aspects are highlighted. Though their conversation centers on mothers and birthing, the young men ignore the off-stage travails of Mina Purefoy. Bloom alone respects the sacred quality of the birthing hour and remains on the sidelines of the merrymaking. The theme of crimes against sacred fertility is highlighted in the controversial topic of birth control.

In Episode Fourteen, for the first time, we see Stephen and Bloom together in a social situation. The two men are both sidelined from the rest of the group. Stephen's musings on religious doctrine are as out of place as Bloom's sincerity and scientific explanations. Both refuse to go home even at this late hour. Bloom is haunted by Molly's actions of the day, while Stephen is haunted by Buck, who shows up halfway through this episode, as he did in Episode Nine, mocks Stephen's philosophizing and captures the attention of the group for himself. Though Stephen and Bloom are equals in their ostracization, we are invited to see them as son and father. Bloom's consciousness is more fully rendered than Stephen's in this episode, and we see that he feels paternal and protective toward Stephen. While questions of birth and labor lead Stephen's mind to sacred versions of creation, the same questions lead Bloom's mind to personal memories of his own dead son. A substitute for Rudy comes not in the guise of Milly (who is figured in this episode as a future mother, not a present daughter), but in the guise of Stephen, about whose emotions Bloom becomes increasingly perceptive in this episode.

## EPISODE FIFTEEN: "CIRCE"

### SUMMARY
Episode Fifteen takes the form of a play script with stage directions and descriptions, with characters' names appearing above their dialogue. The majority of the action of Episode Fifteen occurs only as drunken, subconscious, anxiety-ridden hallucinations.

Near the entrance to Nighttown, Dublin's red-light district, Stephen and Lynch walk toward a familiar brothel. The focus switches to Bloom, nearby. Bloom has attempted to follow Stephen and Lynch to Nighttown, but he has lost them. He ducks into a pork butcher's to buy a late-night snack. Bloom immediately feels guilty about the expense, and a hallucination begins in which Bloom's parents, Molly, and Gerty MacDowell confront Bloom about various offenses. Next, Mrs. Breen appears—she and Bloom briefly renew their old flirtation.

In a dark corner, Bloom feeds his meat purchases to a hungry dog— this suspicious-looking act engenders another hallucination in which

SUMMARY & ANALYSIS

two nightwatchmen question Bloom, who responds guiltily. Soon, Bloom is on public trial, accused of being a cuckold, an anarchist, a forger, a bigamist, and a bawd. Witnesses such as Myles Crawford, Philip Beaufoy, and Paddy Dignam in dog form appear. Mary Driscoll, the former housemaid to the Blooms, testifies that Bloom once approached her for sex.

The nightmarish scene ends as Bloom is approached by prostitute Zoe Higgins. Zoe guesses that Bloom and Stephen, both in mourning, are together. She tells him Stephen is inside. Zoe playfully steals Bloom's lucky potato from his pocket, then teases Bloom for lecturing her on the ills of smoking. Another fantasy ensues, in which Bloom's smoking lecture escalates into a campaign speech. Soon Bloom, backed by Irish and Zionists, is coronated as leader of the new "Bloomusalem." The nationalist hallucination turns sour when Bloom is accused of being a libertine—Buck Mulligan steps forward and testifies about Bloom's sexual abnormalities, then pronounces Bloom a woman. Bloom gives birth to eight children.

The hallucination ends with the reappearance of Zoe. Only a second of "real time" has passed since she last spoke. Zoe leads Bloom inside Bella Cohen's brothel, where Stephen and Lynch are socializing with prostitutes Kitty and Florry. Stephen is pontificating and playing the piano. Florry misunderstands Stephen and assumes he is making an apocalyptic prophecy. An apocalyptic hallucination, Stephen's, ensues. Another hallucinatory sequence, Bloom's, begins with the arrival of Lipoti Virag, Bloom's grandfather, who lectures Bloom about sex.

When Bella Cohen herself enters the room, a long hallucination begins—Bella becomes "Bello," proceeding to master and violate a feminized Bloom, while taunting him about past sins and Boylan's virility. Bello suggests that Bloom's household would be better served without him, and Bloom dies. The hallucination continues—perhaps in Bloom's "afterlife"—with the pristine nymph (from the picture in the Blooms' bedroom) humiliating Bloom for being a dirty mortal. The spell ends only when Bloom confronts the nymph with her own sexuality.

Bloom finds Bella Cohen standing before him—again, only seconds seem to have "really" passed since her entrance. Bloom gets his lucky potato back from Zoe. Bella demands payment from the men, and Stephen gives Bella more than enough money for all three of them. Bloom puts down some of his own money and returns Stephen's overpayment to him, then takes control of all Stephen's money for the evening, since Stephen is drunk.

Zoe reads Bloom's palm and pronounces him a "henpecked husband." Another hallucination ensues, involving Bloom watching Boylan and Molly have sex. Talk turns to Stephen's Parisian adventures and Stephen colorfully describes his escape from his enemies and his father.

Zoe starts the pianola, and everyone except Bloom dances. Stephen spins faster and faster, nearly falling. The rotting ghost of his mother rises up from the floor. Stephen is horrified and remorseful—he asks for confirmation that he did not cause her death. The ghost is noncommittal in response, speaking of God's mercy and wrath. The others notice Stephen looks petrified, and Bloom opens a window. Stephen defiantly tries to dispel the ghost and his own remorse, proclaiming that he will stand alone against those who try to break his spirit. Stephen crashes his walking stick into the chandelier. Bella calls for the police, and Stephen runs out the door. Bloom quickly settles with Bella, then runs after Stephen.

Bloom catches up with Stephen, who is surrounded by a crowd and is haranguing British Army Private Carr about unwanted British military presence in Ireland. Stephen announces his own personal intent to mentally subvert both priest and king. Bloom tries to intervene. Carr, feeling his king has been insulted, threatens to punch Stephen. Edward VII, the citizen, the Croppy Boy, and "Old Gummy Granny," the personification of Ireland, appear to encourage the fight, though Stephen remains distasteful of violence.

Lynch impatiently leaves. Stephen calls Lynch "Judas," the betrayer. Carr knocks Stephen out. The police arrive. Bloom spots Corny Kelleher, who is close with policemen, and enlists his help with Simon's son. Kelleher satisfies the police and leaves. Alone in the street, Bloom bends over the barely conscious Stephen, as an apparition of Rudy, Bloom's son, appears.

### ANALYSIS

Not much "really" happens in Episode Fifteen, though it is the longest. The bulk of the episode consists of hallucinations that actually take place in the real-time span of a second or two. In the first half of the episode, we can distinguish the lengthy hallucinations as emerging from either Stephen's or Bloom's subconscious. Thus Bloom's hallucinations are either persecutory in tone, focusing on sexual guilt, or involve an element of wish-fulfillment, as with the appearance of Josie Breen.

Stephen's hallucinations seem to emerge out of elements of his day, such as the interview with Deasy, and involve Stephen's privately torturous interactions with authority, specifically with ideas about God. Yet the distinctions between Stephen's and Bloom's hallucinations are not sustainable. Stephen's hallucinations involve elements of Bloom's day that Stephen could not know about and vice-versa. Eventually, the apparitions begin to reference earlier scenes and words unseen and unheard by both Stephen and Bloom. It is perhaps more accurate to view the hallucinations of "Circe" as emanating not out of the subconscious of individual characters but out of the subconscious of the novel itself.

Episode Fifteen serves to bring Stephen and Bloom closer together. Bloom has followed Stephen to Nighttown with the intention of somehow protecting him—in the more action-packed second half of Episode Fifteen, Bloom begins to fulfill this intent. Bloom overcomes the paralyzing nature of his own sexual guilt and anxiety about Boylan's sexual prowess to take control of several situations—the payment for the prostitutes, Stephen's money, the dispute with Bella over the broken chandelier, and the attempt to save Stephen from the Carr altercation and suspicious police. Comparatively, Stephen, in the latter half of "Circe," seems drunkenly unaware and emotionally overcome by his hallucinations. (Importantly, Stephen's vision of his dead mother seems to be the only true apparition of "Circe." Thus Stephen responds with real emotion, while Bloom, who has experienced equal trauma, has not reacted as though these things actually happened.)

In the final scenes, Stephen attempts to become intellectually and artistically independent through his rejection of "priest and king" and Ireland (Old Gummy Granny). Yet he is mainly depicted as having been abandoned: by his mother, by his father, by Buck and Haines (who have taken Stephen's key and ditched him), and by Lynch ("Judas"). When Stephen is left knocked unconscious at the end of the episode, with his belongings scattered around him, it is Bloom who is there to act as symbolic father and pragmatic caretaker. This preliminary culmination of the father-son union has the tone not of a cosmic convergence but a wish-fulfillment for Bloom, a fact underscored by Bloom's final hallucination of his dead son, Rudy.

# Episode Sixteen: "Eumaeus"

## Summary

Bloom rouses Stephen and begins walking him to a nearby cabman's shelter for food. On the way, Bloom lectures Stephen about the dangers of Nighttown and drinking with "friends" who desert one. Stephen is silent. The men pass by Gumley, a friend of Stephen's father's. Further down, Stephen is accosted by a down-and-out acquaintance, Corley. Stephen half-seriously advises Corley to apply for Stephen's soon-to-be-vacant post at Deasy's school, then gives him a halfcrown. Bloom is appalled by Stephen's generosity. As they continue on, Bloom reminds Stephen that he has no place to sleep tonight himself now that Buck and Haines have ditched him. Bloom suggests Stephen's father's house and reassures Stephen of Simon's pride in him. Stephen is silent, remembering a depressing home scene. Bloom wonders if he has misspoken in his criticism of Buck.

Bloom and Stephen enter the cabman's shelter, the keeper of which is rumored to be Skin-the-Goat Fitzharris, the getaway-car driver during the Phoenix Park murders. Bloom orders coffee and a roll for Stephen. A red-haired sailor asks Stephen what his name is, then if he knows Simon Dedalus. Bloom is confused by Stephen's noncommittal response. When the sailor begins telling tall tales of Simon Dedalus, Bloom assumes it must be a coincidence.

The sailor introduces himself as D.B. Murphy and begins telling travel stories. He passes around a picture postcard of tribal women. Bloom notes suspiciously that the addressee's name is not Murphy. The sailor's tales remind Bloom of his own unambitious travel plans and of the untapped market of affordable travel for the average man.

The sailor describes seeing an Italian knife a man in the back. At the mention of knives, someone brings up the Phoenix Park murders. Silence descends as the clientele think about the Park murders and glance surreptitiously at the keeper. Murphy shows off his tattoos: an anchor, the number 16, and a profile of Antonio, a friend who was later eaten by sharks.

Bloom notices Bridie Kelly standing outside and ducks his head in embarrassment. Seeing her leave, Bloom lectures Stephen about disease-ridden prostitutes. Stephen shifts the conversation from traffic in sex to traffic in souls. A confused discussion ensues—Bloom talks about simple grey matter, and Stephen talks about theological debates about souls.

Bloom urges Stephen to eat and brings their conversation back to the sailor's tale about the Italian knifer. Bloom agrees that Mediterraneans are hot-tempered and mentions that his wife is half-Spanish. Meanwhile, the other men discuss Irish shipping—the keeper insists England is draining Ireland's riches. Bloom thinks a break with England would be foolish, but he wisely keeps silent. He describes to Stephen the similar scene with the citizen, and his own comeback about Christ also being a Jew, though Bloom reassures Stephen that he (Bloom) is not actually a Jew. Bloom outlines his own antidote to the citizen's combative patriotism: a society in which all men worked and were rewarded with a comfortable income. Stephen is unenthusiastic, and Bloom clarifies that work in Bloom's Ireland would include literary labor. Stephen scoffs at Bloom's plan, which condescends to Stephen—Stephen arrogantly inverts this by insisting that Ireland is important because *it* belongs to *him*.

Bloom silently excuses Stephen's impolite and possibly unstable behavior on account of his drunkenness or his difficult homelife. Bloom thinks again about the providence of their meeting, and imagines writing a *Titbits* piece entitled "My Experiences in a Cabman's Shelter." Bloom's eyes wander the evening *Telegraph,* including an item about Throwaway's Gold Cup victory and one about Dignam's funeral, in which Stephen's name and "M'Intosh" are listed as attendees and his own name is misspelled as L. Boom. Stephen looks for Deasy's letter.

Conversation in the shelter switches to Parnell and the possibility that he is not dead but merely exiled. Bloom thinks of the time he returned Parnell's dropped hat to him in a crowd. Bloom meditates on the theme of the long-lost returned or an impersonator claiming to be the long-lost. Meanwhile, the keeper aggressively blames Kitty O'Shea—Parnell's married mistress—for Parnell's downfall. Bloom's sympathies are with O'Shea and Parnell—Kitty O'Shea's husband was obviously inadequate.

Bloom shows Stephen a picture of Molly. Bloom silently hopes Stephen will abandon his prostitute habit and settle down. Bloom considers himself similar to Stephen, remembering his own youthful socialist ideals. Bloom, his head full of plans for them both, invites Stephen to his house for a cup of cocoa. Bloom pays the bill for Stephen's uneaten fare, and he takes Stephen's arm, as Stephen still seems weak. They begin walking home and chat about music, then usurpers and sirens. Stephen sings an obscure song for Bloom, who considers how commercially successful Stephen could be with his vocal talent. The episode ends with a streetsweeper's view of the two men walking arm in arm into the night.

### ANALYSIS

The third-person narrative of "Eumaeus" is full of overused foreign phrases, clichés, and bungled sayings. It depicts the writing of a bourgeois person attempting to convey a sense of "culture" and failing through lack of literary talent or perhaps late-night fatigue. Accordingly, the fluid persona of the narrator more often picks up Bloom's consciousness than Stephen's, as Bloom in this episode is concerned with keeping up "educated" conversation with his tired partner and conveying a somewhat distinguished persona himself. The error-ridden and banal narrative is the main device by which this climactic meeting of Bloom and Stephen is rendered anticlimactic. Their fated father-son coming-together, which in another book would perhaps be rendered as a perfect union of consciousnesses and souls, is here as boring as the narrative that describes it. Stephen is still drunk and dazed and remains silent for most of the opening of Episode Sixteen. Bloom, far from being the idealized father figure that Stephen needs, appears hypocritical and naggingly overprotective.

Episode Sixteen, "Eumaeus," is the first part of the three-episode postlude of *Ulysses* that is referred to as the "Nostos," which implicitly likens Bloom's night to Odysseus's homecoming to Ithaca. Odysseus disguises himself as an old man to surprise and defeat the usurpers gathered at Ithaca. Before entering the court, Odysseus reveals himself to his son, Telemachus, at the hut of Eumaeus, a swineherd. Because Odysseus returns in disguise, Episode Sixteen is thematically concerned with disguise and false identities. The two main characters, besides Stephen and Bloom, of Episode Sixteen—the keeper of the cabman's shelter and the sailor D.B. Murphy—are shady characters whose true identities are in question. The keeper is rumored to be the legendary "Skin-the-Goat" Fitzharris who drove the getaway vehicle for the Phoenix Park murderers. And Bloom immediately suspects that Murphy, too, is not who he claims to be. Bloom's meditations on the theme of the long-lost returned, or an impersonator returned in his place, reunite the Odyssean theme of the wanderer returned with the theme of disguise-impersonation. Interestingly, it is not Bloom, who is referred to as a "landlubber," but D.B. Murphy (away at sea for seven years), who seems parallel to Odysseus here. This analogy, however, is hardly to be trusted in an episode so concerned with imposters.

Related to its preoccupation with false identities, Episode Sixteen also continues the meditation on rumor and gossip throughout *Ulysses*. In Episode Sixteen, we see the ability of gossip to both exclude people and create a community, as Bloom—until now a subject of rumor—participates in gossip, partially in an attempt to fraternize with Stephen. Rumor further intersects with history in "Eumaeus." The historical event of the Phoenix Park murders (in which the British chief secretary for Ireland and the under-secretary were assassinated in Phoenix Park by a group calling themselves the Irish Invincibles) still generated confusion and rumor more than twenty years later, in 1904. While the Phoenix Park murders offer an example of historical events engendering rumor, the case of Parnell demonstrates rumor engendering historical events. Charles Stuart Parnell, a prominent and effective Irish leader, was on the verge of accomplishing home rule for Ireland when news broke of his long-standing affair with the married Kitty O'Shea. Parnell's career was ruined (as were Ireland's short-term chances for home rule) when he was persecuted by the Irish Catholic Church and public. Though the shadow of Boylan and Molly's affair constantly hangs over him, Bloom sympathizes with the adulterous couple, perhaps because he associates himself with Parnell, another civic-reformer and gentleman.

Bloom erroneously imagines that his preoccupation with civic and political reform gives him something in common with Stephen, but Stephen's rudely cryptic statements are deliberately apolitical. Bloom continues to give Stephen the benefit of the doubt, to be grateful for his company, and to make future plans for their continued acquaintance. The idealistic father-son relation between the two is further undermined here, as Bloom's plans for them reveal the entrepreneurial side of his interest in Stephen.

# EPISODE SEVENTEEN: "ITHACA"

*. . . each contemplating the other in both mirrors of the reciprocal flesh of theirhisnothis fellowfaces.*
(See QUOTATIONS, p. 83)

## SUMMARY
Episode Seventeen is narrated in the third person through a set of 309 questions and their detailed and methodical answers, in the style of a catechism or Socratic dialogue.

Bloom and Stephen walk home chatting about music and politics. Arriving home, Bloom is frustrated to find that he forgot his key. He jumps over the fence, enters through the kitchen, and re-emerges at the front gate to let Stephen in. In the kitchen, Bloom puts the kettle on. Stephen declines Bloom's offer to wash, as Stephen is a hydrophobe. The contents of Bloom's kitchen are reviewed, including those that betray Boylan's presence earlier in the day—a gift basket and betting tickets. The latter remind Bloom of the Gold Cup, and the misunderstanding between himself and Bantam Lyons (in Episode Five) dawns on him.

Bloom serves cocoa for them both, and they drink in silence. Bloom, watching Stephen think, considers his own youthful forays into poetry. The narrative reveals that Bloom and Stephen have met twice before—once when Stephen was five, and another time when he was ten. On the latter occasion, Stephen invited Bloom to dinner at the Dedalus's, and Bloom politely declined. Their personal histories are compared, as well as their temperaments—Stephen's is artistic, while Bloom's tends toward applied science through his interest in invention and advertising.

The two men trade anecdotes, and Bloom considers the possibility of publishing a collection of Stephen's stories. They recite and write Irish and Hebrew for each other. Stephen senses the past in Bloom, and Bloom senses the future in Stephen. Stephen goes on to chant the anti-Semitic medieval story of "Little Harry Hughes," in which a Christian boy is beheaded by a Jew's daughter. Stephen's exposition of the story suggests that he could see both himself and Bloom as the Christian child of the story. But Bloom has mixed feelings and immediately thinks of his own "Jew's daughter," Millicent. Bloom remembers moments from Milly's childhood and, thinking of a potential union between Stephen and Milly (or Molly), invites Stephen to stay the night. Stephen gratefully declines. Bloom returns Stephen's money to him, rounded up one pence, and suggests a variety of future interactions. Stephen seems noncommittal, and Bloom becomes pessimistic. Stephen seems to share Bloom's sense of dejection.

SUMMARY & ANALYSIS

Bloom shows Stephen out, and they urinate together in the yard while looking at the night sky, where a shooting star suddenly appears. Bloom lets Stephen out, and the two shake hands as the church bells ring. Bloom listens to Stephen's footsteps and feels alone.

Bloom goes back in. Entering the front room, he bumps his head on furniture that has been moved. He sits down and begins to disrobe. The contents of the room and Bloom's budget for the day (omitting the money paid to Bella Cohen) are catalogued. Bloom's ambition to own a simple bungalow in the suburbs is described. Bloom deposits Martha's letter in his locked cabinet drawer and thinks pleasantly about his favorable interactions today with Mrs. Breen, Nurse Callan, and Gerty MacDowell. The contents of the second drawer include several family documents, including Bloom's father's suicide note. Bloom feels remorseful, mostly because he has not upheld his father's beliefs and practices, such as keeping kosher. Bloom is grateful for his father's monetary legacy, which saved him from poverty—here Bloom daydreams of his unrealized vagrant self, traveling all over the globe, navigating by the stars.

Bloom's revery ends, and he moves toward his bedroom, thinking of what he did and did not accomplish today. Entering the bedroom, Bloom notices more evidence of Boylan. Bloom's mind skims over his assumed catalogue of Molly's twenty-five past suitors, of which Boylan is only the latest. Bloom reflects on Boylan, feeling first jealous, then resigned.

Bloom kisses Molly's behind, which is near his face, as he is sleeping with his head at the foot of the bed. Molly wakes up, and Bloom tells her about his day with several omissions and lies. He tells Molly about Stephen, whom he describes as a professor and author. Molly is silently aware that it has been over ten years since she and Bloom have had sexual intercourse. Bloom is silently aware of the tenseness of their relations since the onset of Milly's puberty. As the episode comes to a close, Molly is described as "Gea-Tellus," Earth Mother, while Bloom is both an infant in the womb and the sailor returned and resting from his travels. A typographical dot ends the episode and indicates Bloom's resting place.

---

## ANALYSIS

Episode Seventeen, "Ithaca," is often read as the final episode depicting Ulysses' wanderings—the large dot at the end of the episode seems to function as a period to the long sentence that is the novel proper. Yet Episode Seventeen offers no easy or triumphant resolution. The cold, scientific objectivity of the reporting underscores the unfamiliar and untriumphant quality of Bloom's Odyssean homecoming. The narrative style is replete with detail, yet not all the details seem particularly relevant. Thus, just as we reach the climactic episode of Bloom and Stephen's union, the narrative style switches to an encyclopedic narrative—the opposite of a traditionally plotted story in which all information pertains and leads up to a climax and a meaning or moral. Joyce refuses to wrap up the emotional strands of the novel, or to offer a heavy-handed moral. Instead we are left with a consistently ambivalent final view of our two male protagonists.

The final union between Stephen and Bloom is infused with positive symbolic importance through the episode's ritualistic diction and universal motifs of death and creation. Yet the form of the episode, with its itemized narrative style, also highlights Bloom's and Stephen's differences even more succinctly, and the union cannot be said to be a practical success. Though Stephen has begun to sober up and become more personable, the perceived gap between them is reinforced by Stephen's blatantly anti-Semitic story, inexplicably offered after a heartwarming exchange of the Irish and Hebrew languages, in which the two men feel the similarity of their "races." There is evidence that Stephen does not mean for the story to be an aggressive gesture—he seems to use it, as he has many things today, as a kind of parable, indeed, a parable in which both himself and Bloom can be figured as victims and receive redemption. Bloom's and Stephen's failures to consider each other's modes of reception causes the disconnect. Here lies the lesson of Episode Seventeen, to the extent that there is one: any coming-together must also be marked by a recognition of otherness.

Stephen's and Bloom's most successfully close moments in Episode Seventeen reflect this lesson—for example, their sharing of the Irish and Hebrew languages is marked by otherness. Bloom and Stephen both co-opt languages that neither is fluent in to enact this meeting of cultures. And it is at this moment that both, looking at and listening to each other, recognize what is alien in the other—Stephen hears the past in Bloom, and Bloom sees the future in Stephen. This interplay of strangeness and familiarity is again replayed in the garden scene. Joyce exploits this interplay not just in the meeting and parting of Bloom and Stephen, but in the reading experience of Ithaca itself. In the obtusely scientific and literal narrative of the episode, things familiar to us, like a kettle boiling, are made strange. Like Bloom and Stephen, we readers must appreciate what is strange in order to recognize the familiar.

The second half of Episode Seventeen details Bloom's return to his house and his preparation for bed. This corresponds to Odysseus's return to his court, where he slays Penelope's suitors then reveals himself to Penelope, who has slept through the slaughter. Yet upending this heroic dimension, as always, is the prosaic—in Episode Seventeen, Bloom is shown to be most pathetically bourgeois. The fantasy of Bloom as the dark wanderer is tempered by the extensive description of

Bloom's ultimate ambition to own a well-furnished suburban bunga-low. These competing perspectives hold each other in check, and to the extent that Bloom emerges as a hero in the bourgeois context, it is because he is able to replicate the narrative's technique of shifting per-spective. Bloom can pragmatically see himself in the context of a single night's sleep, a lifetime's work, or a universe's lifetime. Bloom bests Boylan through a similarly impressive display of shifting perspective—Bloom contextualizes Boylan not as a equal and immediate rival, but as one of many, not the first nor the last. *Ulysses* dwells on the idea that shifting perspective forces one to question one's own moral judgment. To the extent that Bloom duplicates this practice within himself, he emerges as the hero of the book. As you may imagine, though, there is another perspective on this, and it is Molly's perspective in Episode Eighteen that finally flushes out the biased visions of her that have held precedence thus far.

## Episode Eighteen: "Penelope"

### Summary

> *so he could feel my breasts all perfume yes and his heart was going like mad and yes I said yes I will Yes.*
>
> (See QUOTATIONS, p. 84)

The first of Molly's eight giant "sentences" that comprise her interior monologue begins with her annoyance and surprise that Bloom has asked her to serve him breakfast in bed. Molly intuits that Bloom has had an orgasm today, and she thinks of his past dalliances with other women. She thinks of her afternoon of sex with the aggressive and well-endowed Boylan—a refreshing change after Bloom's strange lovemak-ing techniques. On the other hand, Molly guesses Bloom is more virile than Boylan and remembers how handsome Bloom was when they were courting. Thinking of Josie and Denis Breen's marriage, Molly feels that she and Bloom are perhaps mutually lucky.

In Molly's second sentence, she considers her various admirers: Boy-lan, who likes her feet; the tenor Bartell D'Arcy, who kissed her in church; Lt. Gardner, who died of fever in the Boer War. Molly ponders Bloom's underwear fetish. Aroused, Molly anticipates seeing Boylan on Monday and their upcoming trip to Belfast alone. Molly's thoughts turn briefly to the world of concert singing, annoyingly girlish Dublin singers, and Bloom's help with her career. Molly remembers Boylan's anger over Lenehan's lousy Gold Cup race tip. Molly thinks Lenehan is creepy. Considering future meetings with Boylan, Molly resolves to lose some weight and wishes she had more money to dress stylishly. Bloom should quit the *Freeman* and get lucrative work in an office. Molly remembers going to Mr. Cuffe to plead for Bloom's job back after he was fired—Cuffe stared at her breasts and politely refused.

In her third sentence, Molly ponders beautiful female breasts and silly male genitalia. She thinks of the time Bloom suggested she pose naked for a photographer to make money. She associates pornographic pictures with the nymph picture that Bloom used to ineptly explain metempsychosis this morning. Back to breasts, she remembers how Bloom once suggested they milk her excess breast milk into tea. Molly imagines gathering all of Bloom's outrageous ideas into a book, before her thoughts return to Boylan and the powerful release of her orgasm this afternoon.

Molly's fourth sentence begins with a train whistle. Thoughts of the hot engine car lead her to thoughts about her Gibraltar childhood, her friendship there with Hester Stanhope and Hester's husband "Wogger," and how boring her life was after they left—she had resorted to writing herself letters. Molly thinks of how Milly sent her only a card this morning and Bloom a whole letter. Molly wonders if Boylan will send her a love letter.

Molly's fifth sentence begins with her recollection of her first love letter—from Lieutenant Mulvey, whom she kissed under the Moorish wall in Gibraltar. She wonders what he is like now. Another train whistles, reminding Molly of *Love's Old Sweet Song* and her upcoming performance. She is again dismissive of silly girl singers—Molly views herself as much more worldly. Considering her dark, Spanish looks which she inherited from her mother, Molly guesses that she could have been a stage star if she had not married Bloom. Molly shifts in bed to quietly release built-up gas, chiming with another train's whistle.

In her sixth sentence, Molly's mind wanders from her Gibraltar girlhood to Milly. Molly does not like being alone in the house at night now—it was Bloom's idea to send Milly to Mullingar to learn photography, because he sensed Molly and Boylan's impending affair. Molly ponders her close but tense relationship with Milly, who has become wild and good-looking like Molly used to be. Molly realizes with frustration that her period is starting and gets up to use the chamberpot. She realizes that Boylan did not make her pregnant. Scenes from the afternoon run through her mind.

In her seventh sentence, Molly climbs quietly back into bed and thinks back over their frequent moves, a result of Bloom's shaky financial history. Molly worries that he has spent money on a woman today, as well as the Dignam family. Molly thinks of the men at Dignam's funeral—they are nice, but Molly resents their condescension to Bloom. Molly recalls Simon Dedalus's vocal talent and wonders about Simon's son. Molly remembers meeting Stephen as a child and fantasizes that Stephen is probably not stuck-up, just young enough, and appealingly clean. Molly plans to read and study before he comes again so he will not think her stupid.

In her eighth sentence, Molly thinks of how Bloom never embraces her, weirdly kissing her bottom instead. Molly reflects on how much better a place the world would be if it was governed by women. Considering the importance of mothers, she thinks again of Stephen, whose mother has just died, and of Rudy's death, then stops this line of thought, for fear of becoming depressed. Molly imagines arousing Bloom tomorrow morning, then coldly telling him about her affair with Boylan to make him realize his culpability. Molly makes plans to buy flowers tomorrow, in case Stephen comes. Meditating on flowers and nature, the products of God, she thinks lovingly of the day she and Bloom spent outdoors on Howth, his marriage proposal, and her resoundingly positive response.

---

### ANALYSIS

In Episode Seventeen, we saw Bloom-Odysseus return home and slay his opponents with magnaminity. Episode Eighteen, as the final third of the "Nostos," both calls this triumphant ending into question and ultimately ratifies it. If we read Bloom's final request for breakfast in bed as his reassertion of control of his household, then Molly's indignant reaction to his request unsettles this patriarchal closure. Yet Episode Eighteen also depicts Molly going through the same trial of meeting the suitors-opponents that Bloom enacted in Episode Seventeen. And Molly seems to discard them one by one for Bloom, confirming the triumph of Bloom-Odysseus with her final affirmative "yes."

Early readers of *Ulysses*—preoccupied by the supposed obscenity of Molly's monologue—viewed Molly as the archetypical whore. However, recent focus on the realistic quality of the monologue shows that Molly's character comes across as believably contradictory and nuanced. Her thoughts reveal her to be extremely self-centered, yet she is also shown to be charitable and potentially sympathetic toward others, such as Josie Breen and Stephen. She comes across as uneducated but clever, opinionated, and refreshingly frank. She is hypocritical and self-contradictory but also highly perceptive—she ratifies our negative judgments of some characters, such as Lenehan. Finally, Molly's monologue is highly entertaining—she has a sense of humor and a gift for mimicking the speech of others.

Molly's monologue contains facts and emotions that force us to revise our previous perspective of her and her marriage. For example, Bloom's mental list of Molly's infidelities in Episode Seventeen is here shown to be wildly incorrect—Boylan is Molly's first sexual infidelity, and it has occurred only after more than ten sexless years (and perceived lack of affection) with Bloom. Molly's thoughts offer a new perspective:

it is Bloom who has been compromising her, and his own infidelities call his easy judgment of Molly as unfaithful into question.

However, though Molly gets the final say, her perspective is also dramatized as fallible, specifically through her meditations on Stephen, which are misinformed and idealized. Molly fantasizes about Stephen's humility, friendliness, and cleanliness—three characteristics that do not apply to Stephen as we have seen him. This technique does not demonstrate Molly's individual misperception, as much as the lesson of perspective in *Ulysses*: no single character's perspective will be sufficient to pass judgment. Though Molly's feelings toward Bloom oscillate wildly throughout her monologue, as the episode comes to a close, her thoughts center more on Bloom and Stephen-Rudy and less on Boylan and other suitors. The sexual desire prevalent through her monologue becomes more evidently underwritten with a compatible desire for the intimacy of the family structure. Molly's mental return to the scene on Howth that Bloom has also thought of several times today shows the power of memory to provide a source of continued intimacy between them, even if her final yes may be in reference to Mulvey or Bloom. This uncertainty is characteristic of Joyce's endings, and it serves to remind us that we have witnessed only a single day in the lives of the Blooms—progress may have been made in their estranged marriage, but there certainly was not a complete turnaround. On the other hand, the unrestrained affirmation and joy of the final lines cannot be denied.

# Important Quotations Explained

1.  *Amor matris*: subjective and objective genitive.

This quotation, part of Stephen's inner monologue, appears in Episode Two. *Amor matris* translates to "mother love," a concept that Stephen ponders while giving extra help to his student Sargent. Sargent reminds Stephen of himself at the same age—Stephen was similarly dirty and disheveled, a child only a mother could love. Stephen thinks of "mother love" frequently in *Ulysses*—he contrasts the concrete, bodily reality of a mother's love to the disconnected, tension-ridden relation between a father and a child. In Episode Nine, Stephen calls *amor matris* "the only true thing in life," and skeptically identifies paternity as "a legal fiction." The phrase "subjective and objective genitive" refers to the confusion about the translation of *amor matris*—it can be either a child's love for a mother or a mother's love for a child. This touches on Stephen's difficulties in deciding whether to be an active or a passive being. In Episode Nine, he frames the choice this way: "Act. Be acted on." In the quotation from Episode Two above, we see Stephen trying to understand the ethics and power relations involved in his teacher-student relationship with Sargent in terms of the compassion entailed by "mother love."

2.  History is a nightmare from which I am trying to awake.

This quotation appears in Episode Two, during Stephen's conversation with Mr. Deasy. With Sargent and his class earlier in Episode Two, Stephen was the reluctant teacher, and now Deasy attempts to position him as the pupil. But Stephen blithely maneuvers out of this role by way of a few cryptic statements, such as the one above. Here, Stephen's version of history as a "nightmare" is an explicit challenge to Deasy's conception of history as moving toward one goal (the manifestation of God), and an implicit challenge to Haines's version of history in Episode One as something impersonal and cut off from the present ("It seems history is to blame"). Stephen's conception of history has several meanings. Stephen sees history, and Irish history in particular, as filled with violence—Deasy's and Haines's conceptions of history enable this violence by excluding certain people from history in Deasy's case (those who do not believe in a Christian God) and by absolving those who perpetrate violence from any blame in Haines's case. Stephen's comment also refers to his conception of the tensions between art and history—Stephen sees history as an impossible chaos and art as a way of representing that chaos in an ordered fashion. Finally, Stephen's statement is also an extremely personal one—his own history is something he is trying to overcome. At the opening of *Ulysses,* Stephen is feeling particularly hopeless about the possibility of rising above the circumstances of his upbringing.

3.      —What is it? says John Wyse. —A nation? says Bloom.
        A nation is the same people living in the same place. —By
        God, then, says Ned, laughing, if that's so I'm a nation
        for I'm living in the same place for the past five years.

This dialogue occurs in Episode Twelve, during the confrontation scene at Barney Kiernan's pub. Led by the citizen, the men at Barney Kiernan's explicitly identify Bloom as an outsider, his Jewish-Hungarian roots being incompatible with their essentialist conception of Irishness as a "racial" and Catholic category. Here, Bloom's conception of a nation may seem excessively loose (especially when he backs up several lines later to qualify, "Or in different places"), but Bloom's position on nationality as a self-selected category is part of the triumph of Bloom's compassionate humanism over the violent essentialism of the citizen and others. Ned Lambert's sarcastic response to Bloom here is an example of another way in which Bloom is repeatedly marked as an outsider—the Dublin men with whom Bloom associates are skilled in using mockery and sarcasm to establish authority over others, while Bloom does not use humor in this way.

4.      . . . each contemplating the other in both mirrors of the
        reciprocal flesh of theirhisnothis fellowfaces.

This quotation occurs in Episode Seventeen—it is a narrative description of Stephen and Bloom's wordless interaction in Bloom's garden just before Stephen leaves. Their meeting is in no sense ideal—a father-son connection is not explicitly made, and Stephen declines to stay the night and probably will not see Bloom again. Yet the narrative of Episode Seventeen manages to convey their union as symbolically meaningful, by tapping various themes. This sentence manages to include an optimistic set of thematic connotations: the "recognition" theme from (disguised) Odysseus and Telemachus's meeting in *The Odyssey;* and an idea of the father-son relationship involving versions of the same bodily self ("flesh"). The "reciprocal" aspect of their meeting implies that Stephen has managed to find a medium in the troublesome dynamic of activity-passivity. The "theirhisnothis" narrative play also manages to suggest that the meeting is an ideal balance between a coming-together and a realistic recognition of "otherness."

5.     . . . and then he asked me would I yes to say yes my
        mountain flower and first I put my arms around him yes
        and drew him down to me so he could feel my breasts all
        perfume yes and his heart was going like mad and yes I
        said yes I will Yes.

Molly's final words seem to refer immediately to her memory of accepting Bloom's proposition of marriage during their day spent on Howth. However, the ambiguity of the many masculine pronouns in Molly's monologue also exists here—in the same paragraph, she remembers a similar outdoor scene of love with Lt. Mulvey, and the ambiguity of this seeming affirmation of the Blooms' marriage is typical of Joyce's endings. However, the looseness of Molly's language in these final lines also enacts a combination of the immediate realistic level of the text with the idealistic, symbolic level—Molly's "Yes" here is an unqualified affirmative of natural life and of physical and emotional love.

# KEY FACTS

FULL TITLE
*Ulysses*

AUTHOR
James Joyce

TYPE OF WORK
Novel

GENRE
Modernist novel; comic novel; quest novel

LANGUAGE
English

TIME AND PLACE WRITTEN
Trieste, Italy; Zurich, Switzerland; Paris; 1914–1921

DATE OF FIRST PUBLICATION
Individual episodes were published serially starting in 1918; as a novel, it was first published in 1922

PUBLISHER
First serially in *The Little Review*; as a novel by Shakespeare & Company

NARRATOR
Episodes One, Two, Four–Twelve, Sixteen, and Seventeen feature anonymous narrators. Episode Three features Stephen's thoughts. Episode Thirteen features an amalgamation of anonymous narrator, Gerty MacDowell, and Bloom. Episode Fourteen features a variety of narrators, meant to be representative of the prose styles of historical English authors. Episode Fifteen has no narrator. Molly Bloom is the first-person narrator of Episode Eighteen.

POINT OF VIEW
Episodes One, Two, Four–Eleven, Sixteen, and Seventeen are told from the third-person viewpoint. Episode Three features interior monologue. Episode Twelve is told from the first-person. Episode Thirteen is told from the third and first person. Episode Fourteen is told variously in the third-person and first-person. Episode Fifteen is in play-script form. Episode Eighteen features an interior monologue.

TONE

The narratives of Episodes One through Eight have a straightforward tone. Episodes Nine through Eleven have a self-conscious, playful tone. Episode Twelve has a hyperbolic, belligerent tone. Episode Thirteen has a sentimental tone. Episode Fourteen has an extreme variety of tones, including pious, sensational, and satiric. Episode Fifteen has no narrator and therefore no dominant narrative tone. Episode Sixteen has a tired tone. Episode Seventeen has a scientific tone.

TENSE

Present

SETTING (TIME)

8:00 A.M., June 16, 1904–approximately 3 A.M., June 17, 1904

SETTING (PLACE)

Dublin, Ireland, and its surrounding suburbs

PROTAGONIST

Stephen Dedalus, Leopold Bloom, Molly Bloom

MAJOR CONFLICT

Molly Bloom's infidelity with Blazes Boylan; Stephen Dedalus's search for a symbolic father; Leopold Bloom's desire for a son (his only son died eleven years ago several days after his birth)

RISING ACTION

Bloom leaves his house for the day, sees Blazes Boylan on the street several times, and becomes anxious about Blazes and Molly's four o'clock rendezvous. Bloom is convinced they are going to have sex. Stephen and Bloom go about their day. They pass by each other several times and coincidentally meet at Holles St. Maternity Hospital.

CLIMAX

The first climax could be when Bloom looks after Stephen during Stephen's argument with Private Carr (at the end of Episode Fifteen). The second climax is Bloom's return home to his bedroom to discover evidence of Molly's infidelity and to mentally overcome the threat of Blazes Boylan (Episode Seventeen).

FALLING ACTION

Bloom and Stephen rest at a cabman's shelter (Episode Sixteen), then return to the Bloom residence and have cocoa and talk (Episode Seventeen). Bloom tells Molly about his day and asks her to serve him breakfast in bed (Episode Seventeen). Molly lies awake considering the events of the day and a happy memory from her and Bloom's past.

THEMES
> The quest for paternity; the remorse of conscience; compassion as heroic; parallax or the necessity of multiple perspectives

MOTIFS
> Lightness and darkness; the home usurped; the East

SYMBOLS
> Plumtree's Potted Meat; the Gold Cup horserace; Stephen's Latin Quarter hat; Bloom's potato talisman

FORESHADOWING
> Stephen's and Bloom's compatible dreams set in an Eastern marketplace street

KEY FACTS

# Study Questions &
# Essay Topics

## Study Questions

1.  *Describe Dublin as it appears in* Ulysses. *How does it figure into the novel?*

In one sense, Dublin appears as a metropolis in *Ulysses*. It has the trappings of a large city—a public transportation system, a marketplace district, a harbor, several newspapers, a library, a museum, a court system, a university and so on. These elements all appear in *Ulysses*, and in episodes such as Episode Seven they serve to emphasize the institutional systems that play into Dubliners' daily lives, instead of local or rural concerns. Joyce also emphasizes the feel of the urban space by carefully incorporating the geography of the city. The progress of the characters is relentlessly tracked by street and building names. This technique reaches its climax in Episode Ten, in which the progression of many characters in disparate parts of the city is briefly tracked. Episode Ten creates a sense of the large spatial area of Dublin and the bustle of modern life.

In another, sense, however, Dublin appears to be a small town, especially socially. As Bloom moves around the city all day, he constantly runs into friends and acquaintances, and his acquaintances all seem to know, or know of, each other. News and gossip travel quickly, by word of mouth rather than mechanical means. Politics and press seem to intersect with the personal sphere, for example, when Stephen uses his connections to get Mr. Deasy's letter printed in the evening newspaper. Dublin appears to be not a modern, urban space of anonymity and isolation but a community run by personal interaction and influence.

2.  *Describe how the narrative styles of the first six episodes of* Ulysses *differ from the rest of the novel. How does this effect how one interprets the text?*

The first six episodes of *Ulysses* feature a third-person narrator, with dialogue and interior monologue interspersed. The narrative is realistic and straightforward, but is sometimes hard to distinguish from the interior monologues. The interior monologues attempt to realistically render bits of the stream-of-consciousness of the two main characters, Stephen and Bloom. The focus seems to be on developing and depicting the characteristics of each of these individuals through the ways in which their thoughts work. Thus, several episodes, such as Three and

Five, consist mainly of Stephen's or Bloom's thoughts with very little dialogue or narrative. As the novel progresses, however, the narrative becomes increasingly ambiguous. Some of the later episodes feature first-person narrators with distinctive styles (as in Episode Twelve) or a self-conscious third-person narrative that gestures to the text *as a text* by referencing phrases from earlier episodes (as in Episode Eleven). Narrative devices, such as the genealogy of English literary style in Episode Fourteen, or the question-and-answer technique of Episode Seventeen can somewhat obscure what is "actually" happening with the plot. Consequently, our attention shifts from the characters and their individual trials and motivations to an interpretation of narrative style. We are forced to realize the extent to which style effects *what* can be narrated.

3.  *Ulysses is a novel in which few women appear and even fewer speak. Consequently, much of the thinking about women comes from male viewpoints in the novel. How are Stephen's and Bloom's treatment of women different? How are they similar?*

Stephen's and Bloom's different treatments and understandings of women seem to follow the basic differences in their ages and temperaments. Youthful Stephen does not seem to have much experience with women. We see Stephen interact only with the prostitutes at Bella Cohen's brothel, and we hear of his past relations with the prostitute Georgina Johnson and, possibly, the "virgin" at Hodges Figgis's bookstore whom he remembers in Episode Three. The mature Bloom, on the other hand, is at ease with women and converses with several in a friendly way in *Ulysses*. Bloom thinks of women in a physical way—he often perceives Molly in terms of how she feels or smells. Bloom is attentive to women's appearances, and his sightings of women often spark sexual fantasies or physical reactions. Stephen, on the other hand, thinks of women more often in the course of his aesthetic or religious arguments than in sexual fantasies. The women of his arguments fit easily into "types" (Eve and Ann Hathaway as betrayers, for example) and are defined by those roles, rather than by their appearances.

The two men are similar in their sense of women being mysterious and powerful. Bloom's idea of putting two women writing on a cart as an advertisement and Stephen's story about the woman at the Queen's hotel mysteriously writing words on paper (both in Episode Seventeen) both depend on an innate curiosity about what women hide. Stephen's crediting of Ann Hathaway's role in Shakespeare's artistic life and Bloom's understanding of the sacred nature of childbirth suggest that both men regard women as powerful, if in limited ways. Their parallel appreciations of women as mysterious and powerful are, in fact, not that surprising given that both men are "haunted" by women—Stephen by the ghost of his mother and Bloom by the idea of Molly's infidelity. Finally, both men seem to consider women as subjects of art. In Episode Three, Stephen's memory of the Hodges Figgis "virgin" and his view of a female cocklepicker on the beach combine to form the female subject of the poem he composes. Similarly, Bloom, at the end of Episode Four, considers writing a short story for *Titbits* based on Molly's sayings.

## SUGGESTED ESSAY TOPICS

1. Often, the three protagonists of *Ulysses* are understood in terms of a spectrum, with Stephen and Molly on either end and Bloom's personality combining elements of each. In what ways might Stephen and Molly be similar?

2. If Bloom and Stephen are the "heroes" of *Ulysses,* which characters are their "enemies" and why?

3. Discuss how teaching and learning figure into the novel. Can you pinpoint specific scenes that seem to be about teaching? Does *Ulysses* have an argument about how teaching and learning should work?

4. Can you make a case for Bloom as an artist?

5. How does the concept of home work in *Ulysses*? How do the main characters relate to their real and their ideal homes? Does "home" have a political import?

# REVIEW & RESOURCES

## QUIZ

1.   Who haunts Stephen throughout *Ulysses*?

A. His father     B. His mother     C. Shakespeare     D. Ulysses

2.   What does Stephen perceive Buck to be?

A. Lover          B. Muse           C. Savior          D. Usurper

3.   With whom is Stephen *not* identified?

A. Odysseus       B. Telemachus     C. Hamlet          D. Shakespeare

4.   Which of the following *least* characterizes Bloom?

A. Empathetic     B. Antagonistic   C. Masochistic     D. Optimistic

5.   Which of the following does *not* describe Bloom's reaction to Molly's infidelity?

A. Resignation    B. Jealousy       C. Arousal         D. Anger

6.   According to Stephen, with which character from Hamlet does Shakespeare identify?

A. The ghost      B. Prince Hamlet  C. Claudius        D. Gertrude

7.   Who attacks Bloom in Episode Twelve?

A. Stephen        B. The citizen    C. Boylan          D. Simon

8.   Who fantasizes about Bloom in Episode Thirteen?

A. Boylan         B. Mina Purefoy   C. Molly           D. Gertie MacDowell

9.   What does Bloom request from Molly before going to bed?

A. Breakfast      B. Sex            C. Housekeys       D. Underwear

10.   Who was Molly's first love?

A. Lt. Mulvey     B. Boylan         C. Bloom           D. Lt. Gardner

*The Answer Key appears on page 92.*

# SUGGESTIONS FOR FURTHER READING

## BIOGRAPHY

ELLMANN, RICHARD. *James Joyce.* 1959; revised, New York: Oxford University Press, 1982.

## REFERENCE AND ANNOTATIONS

GIFFORD, DON, with ROBERT J. SEIDMAN. ULYSSES *Annotated: Notes for James Joyce's* ULYSSES. Berkeley: University of California Press, 1988.

## EXPLICATION AND CRITICISM

BUDGEN, FRANK. *James Joyce and the Making of* ULYSSES. 1934. Reprint, Bloomington: Indiana University Press, 1960.

FRENCH, MARILYN. *The Book as World: James Joyce's* ULYSSES. Cambridge, Massachussetts: Harvard University Press, 1976

GILBERT, STUART. *James Joyce's* ULYSSES: *A Study.* 1930. Revised, New York: Vintage Books, 1952.

HART, CLIVE, and DAVID HAYMAN, eds. *James Joyce's* ULYSSES: *Critical Essays.* Berkeley and Los Angeles: University of California Press, 1974.

HAYMAN, DAVID. ULYSSES: *The Mechanics of Meaning.* 1970. Revised, Madison: University of Wisconsin Press, 1982.

KENNER, HUGH. *Ulysses.* 1980. Revised, Baltimore: Johns Hopkins University Press, 1987.

MANGANIELLO, DOMINIC. *Joyce's Politics.* London: Routledge & Kegan Paul, 1980.

ANSWER KEY:
1. B; 2. D; 3. A; 4. B; 5. D; 6. A; 7. B; 8. D; 9. A; 10. A